Harriman's
Money Miscellany
A collection of financial facts and corporate curiosities

Edited by
Stephen Eckett and Craig Pearce

HARRIMAN HOUSE LTD
3A Penns Road
Petersfield
Hampshire
GU32 2EW
GREAT BRITAIN

Tel: +44 (0)1730 233870
Fax: +44 (0)1730 233880
Email: enquiries@harriman-house.com
Website: www.harriman-house.com

First published in Great Britain in 2008
Copyright © Harriman House Ltd

ISBN 13: 9781905641956

British Library Cataloguing in Publication Data
A CIP catalogue record for this book can be obtained from the British Library.

Printed in the UK by the MPG Books Group

'Money is the opposite of the weather. Nobody talks about it, but everybody does something about it.'

Rebecca Johnson

Preface

This is not a serious book. It is a collection of trivia. A compendium of titbits, scraps, crumbs, fragments and morsels of information about money. But that is not to say it is without use.

While other books may address the weighty financial issues of the day, this book answers the perennial questions that people have asked throughout the ages, such as:

What currency did the Flintstones use?

How big is the world's smallest banknote?

Why were handkerchiefs often stolen in the time of Dickens?

Why did Thomas Aquinas disapprove of paying interest on loans?

Which is more expensive shrimps or copper?

How do you spell euro?

Answers to the above (and – if you can believe your luck – even more) are revealed in this book.

This Money Miscellany may not do much for your bank account (in fact, it's already depleted it by a few quid), but it will enrich your soul. And so, while this book may not be serious, it is valuable.

Money Miscellany

Ten richest Americans of all time

With their wealth measured as a percentage of GDP and then converted into current money these are the ten richest US citizens of all time:

Citizen	Wealth	Country with similar GDP
John D. Rockefeller	$192bn	Hungary
Cornelius Vanderbilt	$143bn	Kuwait
John Jacob Astor	$116bn	New Zealand
Stephen Girard	$83bn	Bulgaria
Bill Gates	$82bn	Sri Lanka
Andrew Carnegie	$75bn	Tunisia
A.T. Stewart	$70bn	Libya
Frederick Weyerhauser	$68bn	Croatia
Jay Gould	$67bn	Azerbaijan
Stephen Van Rensselaer	$64bn	Uzbekistan

Hole in the wall

The world's first through-the-wall ATM appeared in 1967, in Enfield, north London.

How animals work

'I know at last what distinguishes man from animals: financial worries.'
Romain Rolland

The ten largest stock market crashes of all time

Wall Street 1929-32	- 89%
US Nasdaq 2000-02	- 82%
Japan 1990-2003	- 79%
London 1973-74	- 73%
Hong Kong 1997-98	- 64%
London 2000-03	- 52%
Wall Street 1937-38	- 49%
Wall Street 1906-07	- 48%
Wall Street 1919-21	- 46%
Wall Street 1901-03	- 46%

On trading commodities

In *The Money Masters*, John Train interviewed the commodity trader Stanley Kroll. The book summarises Kroll's four rules of trading commodities as:

1   Identify a major trend, and decide to make a big move.

2   Put your position in place during reactions against the main trend.

3   Put on smaller additional positions in subsequent reactions.

4   When the trend runs out, reverse the procedure in order to liquidate.

Company listed longest on the NYSE

The Consolidated Edison Company of New York Inc is the company that has been continuously listed on the NYSE for the longest time. It first appeared in 1824 as the New York Gas Light Company.

The Buffett portfolio

In mid-2008 Warren Buffett's Berkshire Hathaway reported it held shares in 39 US publicly traded companies. Of those, the top 10 companies accounted for 80% of the value of the portfolio.

The 10 companies were:

Company	Value of holding ($bn)
Coca-Cola	10.7
Wells Fargo	9.0
Procter & Gamble	7.7
Burlington Northern Sante Fe	6.3
American Express	5.8
Kraft Foods	4.5
Johnson & Johnson	4.4
US Bancorp New	2.2
Wesco Financial	2.1
Moody's	1.8

Cash circulation in the USA

These figures show the quantities of cash in circulation in the United States of America in the 20th century.

1910 $ 3,148,700,000 ($34 per person)

1950 $ 27,156,290,042 ($179 per person)

2000 $ 571,121,194,344 ($2,076 per person)

WWII - Hawaii banknotes

In Hawaii during the Second World War, the United States Treasury Department released special stamped banknotes for the islands as a precaution in case of a Japanese invasion. Had the Japanese invaded and confiscated Hawaiian money it would have been worthless on world markets because of these distinguishable markings.

Brother can you spare a denarius?

The pre-decimalisation United Kingdom penny (240 of which made £1) took its symbol "d" from the Latin word denarius, the Roman "penny".

A gentleman's preference

'Gentlemen prefer bonds.'
Andrew Mellon

Exotic currencies

Currency	Country or area
afghani	Afghanistan
ariary	Madagascar
birr	Ethiopia
dram	Armenia
kip	Laos
kyat	Myanmar
lempira	Honduras
leone	Sierra Leone
lilangeni	Swaziland
loti	Lesotho
manat	Azerbaijan
ouguiya	Mauritania
nakfa	Eritrea
ngultrum	Bhutan
pataca	Macau
pula	Botswana
quetzal	Guatemala
ringgit	Malaysia
rufiyaa	The Maldives
som	Kyrgyzstan
somoni	Tajikstan
taka	Bangladesh
won	South Korea

Two cow illustration of political economy

Christian democracy	You have two cows. You keep one and give one to your neighbour.
socialism (ideal)	You have two cows. The government takes them, puts them in a barn with everyone else's cows and and gives you all the milk you need.
socialism (bureaucratic)	You have two cows. The State takes them and puts them in a barn with everyone else's cows. They are cared for by ex-chicken farmers. You have to take care of the chickens the State took from the chicken farmers. The State gives you as much milk and as many eggs as the regulations say you should need.
capitalism	You have two cows. You sell one and buy a bull. Your herd multiplies, and the economy grows. You sell them and retire on the income.
communism (ideal)	You have two cows. Your neighbours help you take care of them, and you all share the milk.
communism (state)	You have two cows. The State takes both of them and gives you milk.
liberalism	You have two cows. You give them back their milk and let them escape. The cows are then put on the Voter Registration list.
feudalism	You have two cows. Your lord takes some of the milk.
militarism	You head for the hills with your two cows. Declare yourself an independent republic. Start shooting if they come for your cows.

continued...

totalitarianism	You have two cows. The government takes them both, denies they ever existed and drafts you into the army. Milk is banned.
representative democracy	You have two cows. Your neighbours pick someone to tell you who gets the milk.
a French corporation	You have two cows. You go on strike because you want three cows.
an Italian corporation	You have two cows, but you don't know where they are. You break for lunch.
a German corporation	You have two cows. You reengineer them so they live for 100 years, eat once a month, and milk themselves.
an American Republican	You have two cows. Your neighbour has none! So what?
an American Democrat	You have two cows. Your neighbour has none. You feel guilty for being successful. You vote people into office who tax your cows, forcing you to sell one to raise money to pay the tax. The people you voted for then take the tax money and buy a cow and give it to your neighbour. You feel righteous.
a Hindu corporation	You have two cows. You worship both of them.
Enron inspired venture capitalism	You have two cows. You sell three of them to your publicly listed company, using letters of credit opened by your brother-in-law at the bank, then execute a debt/equity swap with an associated general offer so that you get all four cows back, with a tax exemption for five cows. The milk rights of the six cows are transferred via an intermediary to a Cayman Island company secretly owned by the majority shareholder who sells the rights to all seven cows back to your listed company. The annual report says the company owns eight cows, with an option on one more.

What does it cost - pets?

Thoroughbred Gelding horse, 3 years old	£2,000
Horse stable, including installation	£1,200
10 hours of child's riding lessons, London	£229
Pure bred British Bulldog puppy	£2,000
Horsfield tortoise	£99
Magnoy Koi Carp 12" - 14"	£80
Garden carp pond, complete kit	From £200
Budgerigar	£15
Budgerigar cage	£50
Chile Rose tarantula	£14.23
Spider cage	From £30
Ferret, from rescue centre	£5
Ferret cage	£170

"In God We Trust"

"In God We Trust" first appeared on the US two cent coin in 1864, but it was not a requirement for all currency and coins to carry the motto until 1955. At present all denominations of paper money carry the phrase.

Life's essentials

'When I was young I used to think that money was the most important thing in life. Now that I am old, I know it is.'
Oscar Wilde

What's stopping you?

'Empty pockets never held anyone back. Only empty heads and empty hearts can do that.'
Norman Vincent

The World Bank

The World Bank began as the International Bank for Reconstruction and Development, and emerged in 1945 after the Bretton Woods agreement was ratified. Initially, financial assistance was granted to assist countries with economic recovery after WWII. Since this time the focus of the bank has developed, and now it works to ameliorate poverty and relieve the poorest nations of their debt. This work to reduce poverty is manifested in projects to improve the infrastructure of developing countries, and the bank is able to provide financial or technical assistance for these projects.

Despite this slight change in direction, the World Bank still makes funds available for reconstructive work in post-conflict areas, and in countries whose economies are not developed enough to deal with environmental disaster.

*

The bank has 10,000 employees working in more than 100 countries.

*

Around $11bn of loans are approved each year, which countries have 15-20 years to repay.

*

Grants to developing countries are funded by the world's wealthiest countries, who make contributions to a fund operated, and distributed, by the bank.

**

Largest one-day falls in the FTSE 100 index

Date	Drop in value
20 October 1987	- 12.2%
19 October 1987	- 10.8%
10 October 2008	- 8.9%
6 Occtober 2008	- 7.9%
15 October 2008	- 7.2%

Largest one-day falls in the DJIA

Date	Drop in value
19 October 1987	- 22.6%
28 October 1929	- 12.8%
29 October 1929	- 11.7%

Pulp to riches - history of Nokia

The Finnish mobile phone company Nokia started life as a wood-pulp mill in 1865. The town of Nokia emerged with the mill as a large workforce was attracted to the area. The Nokia group (formed in 1967) began to focus on the mobile communication market following the recession of the 1990s.

$

The $ sign was designed in 1788 by Oliver Pollock.

Calculating the Dow Jones Industrial Average

The DJIA is calculated by taking the sum of the prices of all 30 stocks ($\sum p$) and dividing by a divisor (d). A divisor is used so that splits, spinoffs or similar structural changes within companies do not alter the numerical value of the DJIA. When the DJIA began the divisor was simply 30, so the DJIA was just the average stock price of the companies. The present divisor is less than one, meaning the DJIA is larger than the sum of the individual stock prices.

> DJIA formula:
>
> $DJIA = \sum p \div d$

UK lottery grants

Here are some organisations that received lottery grants:

£4,335	Rufford Wood Firing Society
£5,000	Dante or Die
£75,000	Greenpeace
£344,000	Belgrade Theatre Trust (Coventry)
£6,435	HM Prison, Albany
£3,500	Bloodaxe Books
£4,950	European Union Chamber Orchestra
£69,500	Excellence in Crewe
£58,000	The Organic Cookery School Limited

Watch out for leaks

*'Beware of small expenses. Small leaks
can sink a big ship.'*
Benjamin Franklin

Sector profiles of the UK stock market

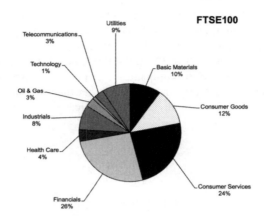

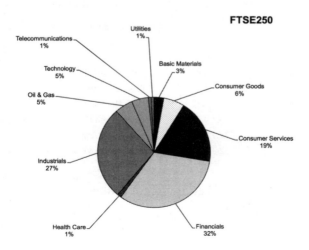

Capital Asset Pricing Model

The Capital Asset Pricing Model (CAPM) is an economic model that describes the relationship between risk and return. The model reflects the theory that higher returns are only possible with higher risks.

$$E(r) = Rf + \text{Beta} \times (E(Rm) - Rf)$$

Where:
E(r) is the expected return rate on a security
Rf is the rate of a risk-free investment
Beta is the volatility of a security in relation to the market
E(Rm) is the anticipated return of the market

The CAPM assumes that investors:

Intend to maximise utilities.

*

Will rationally be averse to risk.

*

Are price takers: they do not influence prices.

*

Can lend and borrow infinitely under a risk free rate of interest.

*

Trade with securities that can be divided into small pieces.

*

Will not incur any transaction or taxation costs.

**

Euro circulation

In December 2006 the euro became the currency with the highest combined cash value in circulation in the world, surpassing the US dollar. At this point there were 610 billion euros in circulation.

Faces on US banknotes

$1..George Washington

$2.............Thomas Jefferson

$5.................Abraham Lincoln

$10.................Alexander Hamilton

$20............................Andrew Jackson

$50...................................Ulysses S. Grant

$100..Benjamin Franklin

Coins in the UK

In the United Kingdom there are an estimated 26bn coins in circulation (430 for each person). On average around 1.5bn new coins are issued every year.

Does money = happiness?

'All I ask is the chance to prove that money can't make me happy.'
Spike Milligan

Historical value of the dollar

This table shows the exchange rate of the dollar against other currencies through the second half of the 20th century.

Currency	1950	1960	1970	1980	1990	2000
British Pound	2.8	2.8	2.4	2.3	1.8	1.5
German Mark	4.2	4.2	3.7	1.8	1.6	2.1
Indian Rupee	4.8	4.8	7.5	7.9	17.5	44.9
Japanese Yen	361.1	360.0	360.0	226.7	144.8	107.8
Swiss Franc	4.4	4.4	4.4	1.7	1.4	1.7

Dear deerskin

The first type of paper note was invented by the Chinese in 118 BC. There was not enough copper available to make the quantity of coins needed and so they used pieces of deerskin to represent a certain value of coins.

You can tell communists by their Marx

'How do you tell a communist? Well, it's someone who reads Marx and Lenin. And how do you tell an anti-communist? It's someone who understands Marx and Lenin.'
Ronald Reagan

Mini-glossary of odd money related terms

Angel investor Describes an investor who invests in a start-up venture.

Dellionaire A person whose wealth is based on owning stock in the Dell Computer Corporation.

Digifeiter Someone who forges money or documents using digital technology.

Entreprenerd Someone who creates an Internet business utilising their programming, engineering, or other technical skills.

Fraud-u-Net Announcing a cutting-edge Internet product or service: a cynical ploy used by companies to raise their stock price.

Get-rich-click Those people who wish to obtain wealth through online investing or by creating an Internet related business.

Hedonic treadmill The principle that a person's economic expectations and desires rise at the same rate as their income, which means greater happiness does not follow from an increased pay-packet.

Joy-to-stuff ratio The ratio of the time a person spends enjoying life against the time they spend buying material items.

Latte factor Describes the frittering away of money on insignificant daily purchases, such as coffee and snacks, which adds up to a large sum over time.

Moon rocket The rapid increase in a company's stock price following an initial public offering.

continued...

Ninja loan A loan or mortgage given to a person who has no income, no job and no assets.

Paint the tape An underhand method used to increase the price of a company's stock. An example would be breaking up a large stock purchase into multiple small purchases to give the illusion of a buying frenzy.

Pecuniary gland A part of the brain of lawyers, doctors and other professionals who bill for their time.

Pump and dump Encouraging investors to buy a particular company's stock in an effort to raise the share price, and thus profiting from an increased stock price by selling shares already owned in that company.

Rio hedge A final effort by an out-of-luck bond trader to recoup losses. This last gamble is hedged by purchasing a one-way ticket to Rio de Janeiro or another distant location.

Spillionaire Someone who profits, as a result of a compensation settlement, from an oil spill.

Stag An investor hoping to benefit from such instances as *Moon rockets*. They purchase shares in a company and look to sell them on again quickly for a profit.

Single-digit midget A company with a share price below $10.

Sidewalk tax Money solicited by, and given to, hawkers and street traders.

Stoozing Borrowing money from a credit card during an initial interest free period, and then investing that for profit.

Trust slug Someone who lives off the proceeds from a trust fund and has grown lazy because of this.

£2 coin inscription

*'If I have seen further it is by
standing on the shoulders of giants.'*

This inscription from the edge of the UK £2 coin is a
citation from a letter written by Sir Isaac Newton in
1676. He was writing to Robert Hooke and used the
phrase to acknowledge the debt he owed to scientists
who had worked before him.

Counterfeit and genuine UK banknotes

The table shows the numbers of each denomination in
circulation in 2007.

	Number of counterfeit notes removed from circulation	Number of genuine notes in circulation (to the nearest 1,000,000)
£5	4,000	235,000,000
£10	6,000	608,000,000
£20	276,000	1,234,000,000
£50	4,000	141,000,000
Total	290,000	2,218,000,000

Disappearance of pre-decimal British coinage

British coinage was decimalised in 1971, but not all pre-decimal coins were removed from circulation at this time. The dates of their demonetisation were:

2/6 Half Crown	1969
1/2p	1969
3d Threepence	1971
1d Penny	1971
6d Sixpence	1980
1/ Shilling	1990
2/ Florin	1993

Money does not grow on trees

Before the First World War the fibres in United States banknotes were made of silk. Nowadays US "paper" currency is printed on a composition of 25% linen and 75% cotton. Added security against counterfeiting is provided by red and blue synthetic fibres of various lengths which run through the banknote.

(If you are planning to launder your money be sure to programme your washing machine for a cotton cycle.)

Cheque this fact

The ancient Romans are believed to have used an early form of cheque, which they called *praescriptiones,* in the first century BC.

Millions and billions

A US Senator reputedly once said 'A billion here, a billion there and pretty soon you're talking about real money.' But for those of us who aren't elected representatives, how big is a million or a billion?

Millions

A million seconds ago it was the middle of the week before last.

A million minutes ago you were two years younger than you are now.

A million hours ago Victoria was Queen of England.

A million days ago this book would have been written in cuneiform.

Billions

A billion seconds ago it was 1959.

A billion minutes ago Jesus was alive.

A billion hours ago our ancestors were living in the Stone Age.

A billion days ago nothing on the earth walked on two feet.

First credit card

The first credit card was issued by American Express in 1958. This was eight years after the first charge card had been issued by Diners Club.

Millions to spend

Based on their expenditure in 2007, how long does it take the governments of the world's five richest countries to spend US$1 million?

USA	12 seconds
Japan	20 seconds
Germany	24 seconds
France	26 seconds
Great Britain	31 seconds

Wages and costs in mid-19th century Britain

Annual wages

Sarah Bernhardt, Coliseum Variety House	1,000 pounds a week
Singer, Canterbury Music Hall	20 pounds a week
Valet	60 pounds
Cook	50 pounds
Coachman	40 pounds
Lady's maid	18 pounds
Nurse maid	17 pounds
Scullery maid	12 pounds

Costs

Seat and five-course meal, Oxford Music Hall	2 shillings, 6 pence
Balcony or stalls seat, Palace of Varieties	1 shilling
Gallery seat, London Palace of Varieties	3 pence
Flat rate fare, City and South London railway 1890	2 pence

Taxpayers' axioms

Matthew Elliott, of the TaxPayers' Alliance, and Lee Rotherham suggested these to be the principle concerns of the taxpayer:

It isn't the government's money, it is the taxpayers' money.

*

Government projects always take longer and cost more than first stated.

*

A problem will rarely be solved by throwing money at it.

*

Improvements to services and a reduction in spending can occur contemporaneously.

*

If it isn't broken the civil service will try to fix it.

*

Less regulation means lower costs for business and more jobs.

*

Managers are paid to manage - they should not need hordes of back-up consultants.

*

Good government is threatened by an "ambulance chasing" legal system.

*

Focussing on targets and quotas distracts from true priorities.

*

More money is soaked up by government as it gets larger.

*

Low taxes create wealth, which generates more tax revenue, which gives a larger budget to be spent where it is needed. High taxes do the opposite.

**

Portraits on Bank of England notes

The following people have appeared on Bank of England notes since 1970.

£1	Isaac Newton 1978-1988
	Duke of Wellington 1971-1991
£5	George Stephenson 1990-2003
	Elizabeth Fry 2002-present
	Florence Nightingale 1975-1994
£10	Charles Dickens 1992-2003
	Charles Darwin 2000-present
	William Shakespeare 1970-1993
	Michael Faraday 1991-2001
£20	Edward Elgar 1999-present
	Adam Smith 2007-present
£50	Christopher Wren 1981-1996
	John Houblon 1994-present

Pound notes withdrawn

Chancellor Nigel Lawson announced in 1984 that pound notes were to be withdrawn from circulation in the UK and replaced with coins.

Rule of 72

The Rule of 72 is used to determine the number of years it will take for an investment or debt to double in value.

For example, if £100 was invested in a compound interest account with interest at 9% per annum:

$$72 \div 9 = 8$$

So, it is estimated it will take 8 years for the investment to double to £200. In practice it would take 8.0432 years, so the rule is fairly accurate.

Table of values to test the accuracy of the rule:

Rate of interest (%)	Actual years	72 rule estimate
0.25	277.61	288.00
0.5	138.98	144.00
1	69.66	72.00
2	35.00	36.00
3	23.45	24.00
4	17.67	18.00
5	14.21	14.40
6	11.90	12.00
7	10.25	10.29
8	9.01	9.00
9	8.04	8.00
10	7.27	7.20
11	6.64	6.55
12	6.12	6.00
15	4.96	4.80
18	4.00	4.00

The country of Los Angeles

If Los Angeles County was a country, it would have the 19th largest economy in the world.

Value for money

'Money often costs too much.'
Ralph Waldo Emerson

Bad companies are good for you

The table below shows the results of research by Eugene Fama and Kenneth French into the behaviour of growth and value stocks.

Annualised Return: 1926-2000

Large Value Stocks	12.87%
Large Growth Stocks	10.77%
Small Value Stocks	14.87%
Small Growth Stocks	9.92%

The figures above demonstrate that value stocks (bad companies) out-perform growth stocks (good companies).

First company traded on the NYSE

The first company traded on the NYSE was the Bank of New York, in 1792. It is still traded today, but has not been listed continuously since the 18th century.

Millionaire

The word millionaire was first used by Benjamin Disraeli in his 1826 novel *Vivian Grey*.

Company profiles

Index	FTSE 100	FTSE 250	Small Cap
Number of companies	100	250	302
Average turnover (£m)	8,553	774	151
Five year turnover growth (%)	70	90	134
Companies making profit (%)	98	81	57
Five year profit growth (%)	261	219	245

The sixth sense

'Money is like a sixth sense without which you cannot make a complete use of the other five.'
W. Somerset Maugham

Bank of England sobriquet

The Bank of England is otherwise known as the Old Lady of Threadneadle Street.

World tax rates

Country	Income Tax	Corporation Tax	VAT
Brazil	34%	15-27.5%	17-25%
China	25%	5-45%	17%
France	33%	10-50%	5.5% or 19.6%
Germany	30%	15-45%	7 or 19%
India	30-40%	10-30%	12.50%
Italy	33%	23-43%	20%
Japan	30%	5-40%	5%
Russia	24%	13%	0, 10 or 18%
UK	21-28%	0, 20 or 40%	17.50%
USA	15-39% (federal) 0-12% (state)	0-35% (federal) 0-10% (state)	0-10%

Economic systems

agorism	Agorism is similar to anarcho-capitalism, with a revolutionary flavour. The ultimate target is to create a society in which "all relations between people are voluntary exchanges - a free market".
anarchism (left)	Anarcho-syndicalists and anarcho-communists reject capitalism because it is intrinsically bound up with systems of authority.
anarchism (right)	Anarcho-capitalists endorse unfettered capitalism as a system which generates freedom.
capitalism	An economic system where the means of production, distribution and exchange are privately owned and operated through a free market.
communism	Typified by the rejection of private property and class structure, a system where the means of production are commonly owned, and distribution is based according to need, rather than want.
corporatism	A series of unelected, hierachical assemblies represent different groups in society, and run the economy by dictating policy in their area of expertise.
Georgism	Each person owns what they create with their own hands, but things occuring naturally are commonly owned.

continued...

laissez-faire	It is debated whether this has ever existed, but the ideal is that the economy is best served by government taking a back seat and individuals being given free reign in business affairs.
market socialism	A socialist system where state or local planners direct the economy.
mercantilism	The principle that the wealth of a state depends upon the capital it controls within a global economy where the volume of trade cannot be changed.
protectionism	Government or the directors of the economy impose restrictions to limit trade between states, ie, tariffs, exchange rate manipulation and maximum quotas for imports/exports.
socialism	Generally defined by a wish to see greater equality of economic outcome in society, sometimes by giving the workers more control of the means of production, and usually involving state direction of the economy.
syndicalism	Worker's unions and organised labour are the most important features of a syndicalist society. It is believed by syndicalists that capitalism can be weakened, and society organised in the interests of the majority, if labour unions run the economy.
third way	A mix of free-market and state directed economics. Competition, education and technological advances are all important.

The debt of nations

Debt as a percentage of a country's GDP.

Country	Debt
Zimbabwe	212%
Japan	196%
Lebanon	187%
Seychelles	144%
Jamaica	127%
Egypt	106%
Italy	104%
Singapore	101%
Sudan	99%
Greece	90%

Hungarian 100 Million B-Pengo

The largest banknote ever released, in terms of its denominational value, is the 100,000,000,000,000,000,000,000 Pengo. When issued in Hungary in 1946 it was worth about US$0.20.

50p and the seven sides

The British 50p coin, introduced in 1969, was the world's first seven-sided coin.

Effect of US presidents on UK markets

Performance of the FT All-Share index during the offices of US presidents.

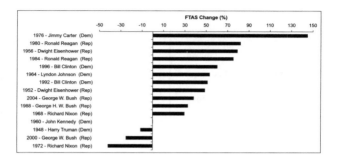

Euro grammar

In English, it would be normal for the words euro and cent to be euros and cents in the plural form, but in official documents the plurals do not take the "s". However, it has been advised by the European Directorate-General for Translation that in documents directed towards the English-speaking general public euros and cents should be used (presumably so that we don't get confused).

What use is economics?

'Economics is extremely useful as a form of employment for economists.'
John K. Galbraith

Ten highest inflation rates

Countries with the highest rates of inflation (December 2007).

Zimbabwe	10,453%
Burma	34%
Guinea	23%
São Tomé and Príncipe	20%
Sri Lanka	20%
Venezuela	19%
Iran	18%
Ethiopia	17%
Democratic Republic of the Congo	17%
Azerbaijan	17%

Wall Street

A five-metre high defensive wall of logs, erected in 1653 to protect New Amsterdam from British colonists, formerly stood where the financial hub of Wall Street is now found.

President against taxation

'Collecting more taxes than is absolutely necessary is legalised robbery.'
Calvin Coolidge

Take a million coins

The respective height, weight and length of UK coins when one million of them are weighed, stacked or lined up.

Coin	Weight	Height	Time
1p	39	32	59
2p	74	36	76
5p	34	33	53
10p	68	36	72
20p	53	33	63
50p	84	35	81
£1	100	61	66
£2	125	49	84

Weight: Given in terms of how many Mervyn Kings (at 85kg each) the coins would weigh.

Height: Given in number of Nelson's columns.

Time: Given in terms of the time taken, in minutes, for a marathon runner to run the length of the line of coins, if they run at the world record pace of 20km/h.

German national currency

The German states were unified in 1871, and this is when Germany first had a national currency (the Mark). Changes have been frequent since this time. Following the First World War the Rentenmark, and then the Reichsmark, were introduced. After the Second World War these were replaced by the Deutschemark and Ostmark. Most recently, the euro was introduced in 1999.

Wealthiest countries

Countries with the highest GDP per capita (2007).

Country	GDP per capita
Qatar	$80,900
Luxembourg	$80,500
Norway	$53,000
Brunei	$51,000
Singapore	$49,700
USA	$45,800
Ireland	$43,100
Switzerland	$41,100
Kuwait	$39,300
Andorra	$38,800

Tons of ink

The facilities that print banknotes in the USA, located at Fort Worth in Texas and in Washington, DC, use approximately 18 tons of ink per day.

A pocketful of coins

If you have one of each of the coins and notes in circulation in the UK you will have £89.88.

On burrowed time

The NASDAQ stock exchange was closed for a day in December 1987 when a squirrel burrowed through a telephone line.

Cost of money

In 2007 it cost approximately 6.2 cents per note to produce the 9.1bn paper currency notes printed in the United States.

Least wealthy countries

Countries with the lowest GDP per capita (2007).

Togo	$800
Central African Republic	$700
Niger	$700
Sierra Leone	$700
Somalia	$600
Guinea-Bissau	$500
Burundi	$400
Libera	$400
Democratic Republic of the Congo	$300
Zimbabwe	$200

Lifespans of currency in the USA

A $1 bill can expect to be in circulation for 21 months.

$5 bill	16 months
$10 bill	18 months
$20 bill	24 months
$50 bill	54 months
$100 bill	90 months

The average lifetime of a coin is 25 years.

Four signs of hyperinflation

People keep wealth in non-monetary assets or convert it to a foreign currency. Any local currency held is invested immediately to maintain any value.

*

Values of goods and money are given in a foreign currency and not the local currency.

*

Sales and purchases on credit are valued at prices that compensate for the expected decrease in value of the currency during the credit period.

*

Cumulative inflation over a three year period approaches, or exceeds, 100%.

**

Weighted dollars

If you stack one million $1 bills the pile will reach 110 metres high and weigh 1 ton.

*

A million dollars' worth of $100 bills weighs 10kg.

*

A million dollars' worth of one cent coins weighs 246 tons.

**

Twentieth century boom and bust periods

In his 2001 article for *Fortune* magazine, Warren Buffett divided the 20ᵗʰ century into six periods of economic activity.

1900-20	Stagnation: the market rose by 0.4% each year.
1921-29	Boom: the Dow rose 430%.
1930-48	Decline: the Dow's value decreased by half over 19 years.
1949-64	Boom: a 500% increase in the market.
1965-81	Stagnation: the Dow gained 0.001% over 17 years.
1982-2000	Boom: bullish market, with a 15-fold increase in value.

Company name changes

Abbey National plc	Abbey plc
Bass plc	Six Continents plc
British Aerospace plc	BAE SYSTEMS plc
British Biotech plc	Vernalis plc
British Gas plc	BG plc
British Steel plc	Corus Group plc
British Telecommunications plc	BT Group plc
BTR Siebe plc	Invensys plc
Burton Group plc	Arcadia Group plc
CGNU plc	Aviva plc
Citigroup	Citi
Commercial Union plc	CGU plc
Cowie plc	Arriva plc
Exco plc	Intercapital plc
FI Group plc	Xansa plc
GEC plc	Marconi Corporation plc
Grosvenor Inns plc	The Slug and Lettuce Group plc
Guinness plc	Diageo plc
Iceland Group plc	The Big Food Group plc
Ladbroke Group plc	Hilton Group plc
National Power plc	Innogy Holdings plc
Trocadero plc	Chorion plc
Unigate plc	Uniq plc
Yorkshire Water plc	Kelda Group plc

Taking a gamble

When investing bear in mind this advice from William T. Ziemba, applied from the world of gambling:

*

Only bet when you have an edge.

*

Those who win on every trade are losers or liars. Making a profit involves taking small losses.

*

Know what you expect to gain from a trade before you enter, and know your exit point.

*

Do your research. The markets are predictable, but use the most contemporary data in models to achieve the best results.

*

Correlations between stocks and bonds are situational, and will not be replicated in all circumstances.

*

Evaluate the impact of all possible scenarios.

*

Have deep pockets - you need enough cash in reserve to survive crises.

*

Accept small losses and exit before losses become too big.

*

Follow a risk control system. If you focus on not losing, rather than on winning, you are more in control.

**

Tips for success in market investing

Inspired by Warren Buffett.

Invest in businesses which you thoroughly understand.

*

Invest only in companies whose future cash flow is certain.

*

Invest only in companies whose returns are anticipated to be above average.

*

Invest only if you can buy shares for less than they are worth.

*

Invest with value in mind, not price.

*

Invest with the long term in mind, do not take notice of short term sentiment.

*

Do not churn your portfolio - stick with your investments.

*

Learn from your mistakes and do not make them again.

**

London Stock Exchange motto

The motto of the London Stock Exchange is:

Dictum Meum Pactum

(My word is my bond.)

What news moves markets?

Research carried out by the Federal Reserve Bank of New York in 2008 found that only a few economic announcements - the nonfarm payroll numbers, the GDP advance release and a private sector manufacturing report - have "significant and persistent effects" on financial markets. According to them, "Most of the other data releases examined generate only transitory or erratic responses."

(The lesson: switch off the screens, forget the newspapers and go to the beach.)

Share price theorem

'Share prices follow the theorem: hope divided by fear minus greed.'
Dominic Lawson

Dollar bill pyramid

The peculiar pyramid image on the $1 bill is designed to signify permanence and strength. The pyramid is unfinished to suggest future growth, and an eye is included to represent a deity watching over the USA.

Printed UK banknotes

Up until 1853 one of the cashiers at the Bank of England signed each individual banknote in circulation. This process ended, and these days 100% of banknotes are printed.

UK stock market weeks

Historically, certain weeks of the financial year have seen markedly better or worse stock market performance than others. Since 1970, the strongest two weeks for the market have been the penultimate and the last trading weeks of the calendar year - week 51 and 52. The market increased in week 51 in 78% of years, and increased in week 52 in 83% of years.

The worst week for the market is week 48.

Marxist economic theory

'Money frees you from doing things you dislike. Since I dislike doing nearly everything, money is handy.'
Groucho Marx

UK market in US election years

These six charts show the performance of the UK market in the years when six recent presidents won election to the White House. The election took place in November in each case.

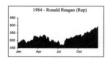
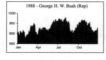
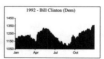

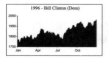
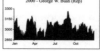
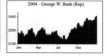

Tulipomania

In *Extraordinary Popular Delusions and the Madness of Crowds* Charles Mackay relates:

"In 1634, the rage among the Dutch to possess [tulips] was so great that the ordinary industry of the country was neglected, and the population, even to its lowest dregs, embarked in the tulip trade."

He gives the example of one particular tulip bought for the following:

	florins
Two lasts of wheat	448
Four lasts of rye	558
Four fat oxen	480
Eight fat swine	240
Twelve fat sheep	120
Two hogsheads of wine	70
Four tuns of beer	32
Two tuns of butter	192
One thousand lbs of cheese	120
A complete bed	100
A suit of clothes	80
A silver drinking-cup	60
Total	2,500

Introduction and demonetisation of British coinage

Coin	Introduced	Demonetised
£2 (old)	1986	
£2	1997	
£1	1983	
50p (large)	1969	1998
50p (small)	1997	
20p	1982	
10p (large)	1968	1993
10p (small)	1992	
5p (large)	1968	1990
5p (small)	1990	
2p	1971	
1p	1971	

Lincoln's right

The one cent coin depicting Abraham Lincoln is the only US coin on which the figure faces right.

1929 all over again

'I'm sure a crash like 1929 will happen again. The only thing that one doesn't know is when. All it takes for another collapse is for the memories of the last insanity to dull.'
John K. Galbraith

The invisible hand

The role of Adam Smith's invisible hand has been an issue of fierce debate for economists and politicians. In his *Wealth of Nations* Smith makes specific reference to an "invisible hand" only once, in this passage:

"By preferring the support of domestic to that of foreign industry, [the merchant] intends only his own security; and by directing that industry in such a manner as its produce may be of the greatest value, he intends only his own gain, and he is in this, as in many other cases, led by an invisible hand to promote an end which was no part of his intention. Nor is it always the worse for the society that it was no part of it. By pursuing his own interest he frequently promotes that of the society more effectually than when he really intends to promote it."

Bucks

Dollars are nicknamed "bucks" in the USA because in trades between native Americans and European settlers buckskin was used as a medium of exchange.

Two Kings' heads are not worth a crown

In 1797, owing to a desperate shortage of silver coins, the Bank of England issued altered foreign coins from its reserves. Half a million pounds worth of Spanish dollars issued by King Charles IV were over-stamped with a small engraving of George III. The re-issued coins, with a value of 4 shillings and 9 pence, attracted ridicule. "Two Kings' heads are not worth a crown" was one witticism.

Ten most expensive regions of the UK

Based on average house price.

Windsor and Maidenhead
Surrey
Greater London
Buckinghamshire
Wokingham
Hertfordshire
Mid Ulster
Oxfordshire
Rutland
Coleraine/Limavady/North Coast

More than a dollar

There are ten currencies with a greater unit value than the dollar.

Country	Unit of Currency	US$ per one unit of currency
Kuwait	dinar	3.73
Bahrain	dinar	2.65
Oman	rial	2.60
Latvia	lats	2.25
United Kingdom	pound	1.49
Jordan	dinar	1.41
European Union	euro	1.27
Azerbaijan	manat	1.23
Cayman Islands	dollar	1.20
Cuba	peso	1.08

Market value of publicly traded shares

Value US$bn	Country
17,000	United States
4,737	Japan
4,477	China
3,058	United Kingdom
2,970	Hong Kong
1,710	France
1,481	Canada
1,322	Russia
1,221	Germany
1,051	South Korea

Taxation as a proportion of GDP

Country	Proportion of GDP (%)
Sweden	54
Denmark	49
Finland	47
Belgium	46
France	45
Austria	44
Italy	42
Netherlands	41
Norway	40
Germany	38

Military spend

Top ten countries by military expenditure (% of GDP).

11	Oman
10	Qatar
10	Saudi Arabia
9	Iraq
9	Jordan
7	Israel
7	Yemen
7	Armenia
6	Eritrea
6	Macedonia

The long-running fiver

The £5 is the denomination of UK banknote that has been present in circulation the longest. It first appeared in 1793.

Santa Claus rally

Not an annual fancy dress motor race, but in fact the name given to a customary rise in the markets in December, and especially in the last week of the calendar year.

Selected episodes of hyperinflation

Country	Impact
Angola 1991-1995	1 new kwanza (1999) = 1,000,000,000 1991 kwanzas.
Argentina 1975-1991	1 peso (1992) = 100,000,000,000 1983 pesos.
Georgia 1994	1 lari (1995) = 1,000,000 1993 kuponi.
Germany 1923	Prices doubled every 48 hours. Rentenmark (1923) = 1,000,000,000,000 1922 Marks.
Greece 1944	Inflation reached 8.5bn% per month. Prices doubled every 28 hours. 1 drachma (1953) = 50,000,000,000,000 1943 drachmai
Nicaragua 1987-1990	1 córdoba (1991) = 50,000,000,000 1987 córdobas
Peru 1984-1990	1 nuevo sol (1991) = 1,000,000,000 1984 soles de or
Poland 1990-1993	1 new zloty (1994) = 10,000 old (1990) zlotych

Daily timetable of the UK market

07h00	Regulatory news service opens
07h50-08h00	Pre-market auction
08h00	UK market and FTSE 100 Index Futures open
08h00-16h30	Continuous trading
14h30	US markets open
16h30-16h35	Post-market auction
17h30	FTSE 100 Futures close
18h30	Regulatory news service closes

Pound coin designs

Year	Design
1983	Ornamental royal arms
1984	Thistle, coronet
1985	Leek, coronet
1986	Flax, coronet
1987	Oak tree, coronet
1988	Crown and shield
1994	Lion rampant
1995	Welsh dragon
1996	Celtic Cross, pimpernel
1997	Three lions
2004	Forth Bridge
2005	Menai Suspension Bridge, Wales
2006	MacNeill's Egyptian Arch, Belfast
2007	Millenium Bridge, Newcastle
2008	Royal coat of arms

Industrial production

Growth in industrial production includes expansion in the manufacturing, mining and construction industries.

Top ten countries for industrial production growth:

Growth rate (%)	Country
30	Sudan
25	Azerbaijan
24	Angola
17	Slovakia
17	Vietnam
14	Bulgaria
13	China
13	Rwanda
13	Georgia
12	Uzbekistan

Watering stock

The notion of a watered stock being one that is over-valued quite possibly derives from a time when farmers would feed their cattle salt, to encourage them to drink water, before putting them up for sale.

Shopping for bargains

'Buy stocks like you buy your groceries, not like you buy your perfume.'
Warren Buffett

Stock market goes over the moon

Lunar eclipses occur when the earth passes between the sun and the moon (they can only occur at full moons).The chart shows the FTSE 100 index and the occurences of lunar eclipses (the vertical bars) since 2000.

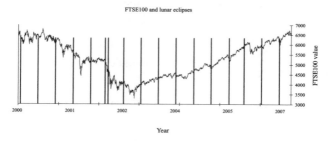

FTSE100 and lunar eclipses

Year

The average daily change of the FTSE 100 index is +0.04%. However, on full moon days the average increase is three times greater, at +0.128%.

	All days	Full moon days
Average daily change	0.04%	0.128%
Number of days with an increase	51.4%	58.1%

Money's little irony

'One of the strange things about life is that the poor, who need money the most, are the very ones that never have it.'
Finley Peter Dunne

The development of private wealth in Britain

In *The Richest of the Rich* Philip Beresford and William D. Rubinstein presented this timetable for the development of wealth in Britain.

1066-90	William the Conqueror rewards his followers with large estates around England.
c1193	The City of London had semi-independent status at this time, and had already emerged as an important commercial centre.
1216-63	Eight mercantile families, connected by marriage, produced 45 aldermen.
1327	City of London no longer subject to direct royal interference.
1361	First fortune of £100,000, accrued by the Duke of Lancaster.
1610	First business fortune of £500,000, earned by Sir John Spencer.
1720	First millionaire - James Brydges, Duke of Chandos.
1833	First business fortune of £5m, earned by the First Duke of Sutherland.
1883	Another £5m businessman - Baron Overstone.
1899	The Duke of Westminster dies, leaving behind £14m.
1917	Sir John Ellerman reports his fortune to be £37m. His business was finance and shipping.
1969	William Morris, Lord Nuffield, the automobile manufacturer, dies leaving a fortune of £3.5m having already given a reported £36m to charity.
1980s	The *Sunday Times* rich lists emerge, giving greater publicity to the wealthy. The richest at this time are billionaires.
2005	Laksmi Mittal amasses the first British fortune of £10bn, and improves this to nearly £20bn by 2007.

The six-month effect

There is a theory that stocks fare better in the period November to April than in the six month period beginning with May.

There appears to be some truth to this, because the UK market data indicates that five of the six traditionally best trading months are between November and April inclusive.

This has given rise to the aphorism:

'Sell in May and go away, don't come back until St. Leger's Day.'

ATM

ATM is short for Automatic Teller Machine, but why use this name for a hole in the wall which dispenses money and account information?

The French word *aconter* means "tell" and is, along with *acompter*, meaning count, the source of the English word account or accounting.

An Automatic Accounting Machine then.

Time to sell

'When good news about the market hits the front page of the New York Times, sell.'
Bernard Baruch

Mark Twain effect

The Mark Twain effect is the supposed occurence of lower stock returns in October than in any other month. This is drawn from his book *Pudd'nhead Wilson*, where it is asserted:

'October. This is one of the peculiarly dangerous months to speculate in stocks. The others are July, January, September, April, November, May, March, June, December, August, and February.'

The effect is belied by the information about the UK markets below - October is actually the third best month.

Monthly performance of the UK stock market

Month	% of years the market rises in this month	Average market change in this month (%)
April	79	2.8
December	70	2.2
October	70	0.3
January	68	2.7
August	65	1.3
November	65	0.6
March	63	0.7
July	55	0.3
February	53	1.4
September	46	- 1.3
June	45	- 0.8
May	45	- 0.5

Habits for successful investors

In *The Harriman Book Of Investing Rules* Dean LeBaron suggests the following habits for successful investors:

Ignore earnings and follow the cash.

*

Be aware that corporate control is worth everything or nothing, and no point in between.

*

Learn more about enterprises from competitors than the enterprises themselves.

*

Avoid company visits since they are usually successful promotions.

*

Commercial bankers usually know the inside story and are a source of hints.

*

Ignore the advice and issues of investment bankers.

*

Prestige is inversely related to future investment success.

**

Singing from the same hymn sheet

'When it's a question of money, everybody is of the same religion.'
Voltaire

Euro notes

Note	Number of notes in circulation in 2008 (m)	Value in circulation (€m)
€500	464	232,238
€200	157	31,385
€100	1,215	121,486
€50	4,292	214,614
€20	2,335	46,697
€10	1,856	18,560
€5	1,368	6,841
TOTAL	11,687	671,821

Where the world's poor live

Ten countries with the greatest proportion of the world's poor. For example, India is home to 41% of the world's poor.

Country	Proportion (%)
India	41
China	22
Nigeria	8
Pakistan	4
Bangladesh	3
Brazil	2
Ethiopia	2
Indonesia	1
Mexico	1
Russia	1

Euro coins

Coin	Number of coins in circulation in 2008 (m)	Value in circulation (€m)
€ 2	3,851	7,702
€ 1	5,793	5,793
50 cent	4,677	2,338
20 cent	8,031	1,606
10 cent	10,153	1,015
5 cent	12,670	634
2 cent	14,721	295
1 cent	18,035	180
TOTAL	77,931	19,563

Most international stock exchange

The London Stock Exchange became the world's most varied stock exchange in November 2007, in terms of the range of countries represented among its markets. At this time 3287 companies from more than 60 countries had been admitted to trade on the LSE.

Britain's national currency

A single British national currency was established in 928AD following the Statute of Greatley.

ATMs dispensing euros

Number of ATMs	Country
60,372	Spain
53,887	Germany
43,700	France
40,058	Italy
12,378	Portugal
7,614	Austria
7,556	Netherlands
7,256	Belgium
6,258	Greece
3,306	Ireland
1,669	Finland
1,643	Slovenia
404	Luxembourg
246,101	Total

What affects the market?

'The thing that most affects the stock market is everything.'
James Playsted Wood

Rich states of America

Richest US states by GDP, and countries with a similar GDP.

State	GDP (US$bn)	Similar country
California	1,813	Italy
Texas	1,142	Turkey
New York	1,103	Indonesia
Florida	734	Taiwan
Illinois	610	Saudi Arabia
Pennsylvania	531	Argentina
Ohio	466	Pakistan
New Jersey	465	Egypt
North Carolina	399	Belgium
Georgia	397	Malaysia

California truly earns its nickname of the Golden State in terms of total wealth then, but it does not have the highest GDP per capita. This honour goes to Delaware, aptly monikered the First State, with a GDP per capita of $56,496.

Bizarre company names

Apparent Networks, Blue Gecko, BreakingPoint
Systems, Cavalier Telephone, Chumby, Dimdim, DORC,
Eblana Photonics, Flytxt, Gigle, Global Vibration,
HitTail, Hurray!, Men & Mice, Pelephone,
Communications, Podaddies, Render Vanderslice,
TellyTopia, Voxbone, Wapple

Quick facts about quick cash

There are more than 60,000 cash machines in the UK.

*

There were 2.75bn withdrawals from cash machines in
2006, an average 87 each second throughout the year.

*

The average withdrawal from ATMs in 2006 was £66.

*

35.1m people were regular users of cash machines in
2006, with each person making 78 withdrawals
throughout the year. On average each person withdrew
£100 a week from ATMs.

*

164.1m cards that could be used in cash machines were
in issue in the UK by the end of 2005.

*

The total value of all withdrawals from cash machines in
2006 was £180bn.

**

FATF blacklist

The Financial Action Task Force blacklist is produced to indicate which countries do not make acceptable attempts to combat money laundering and terrorist financing, or which countries are unable to do so. These countries are referred to as non-cooperative countries and territories (NCCTs).

*

The first report in June 2000 included the following:

Bahamas, Cayman Islands, Cook Islands, Dominica, Israel, Lebanon, Liechtenstein, Marshall Islands, Nauru, Niue, Panama, Philippines, Russia, St. Kitts and Nevis, St. Vincent and the Grenadines

*

The most recent list that had any entries was released in June 2006, with Myanmar being the only state listed. Myanmar was then delisted by the FATF in October 2006, and since that time the list has been empty.

**

Bowie bonds

In January 1997 David Bowie made musical and financial history when he raised $55 million by issuing 10-year asset-backed bonds. The collateral for the bonds came from the future royalties he expected to earn on the back catalogue of albums he recorded before 1990. The bonds were bought by Prudential Insurance Co.

Slow day at the NYSE

On 16 March 1830, only 31 shares changed hands at the NYSE. It is the slowest day in the exchange's history.

*

The most active day was 16 August 2007, with 5,799,792,281 shares traded.

Five flag theory

WG Hill's five flag theory suggests breaking one's life into five compartments, contained in five different countries or states, to achieve economic and personal freedom.

1   Register passport and citizenship in a country that does not charge tax on incomes earned outside the country.

2   Have your legal residence in a tax haven.

3   Earn your money in a country of state that has low corporation tax rates.

4   Keep your money in banks or assets in a country with low taxation of savings interest and low capital gains taxes.

5   Spend your money in a country or area that has low rates of VAT and consumption tax.

Medieval shopping list

Presented below is a selection of costs for everyday goods, as presented in the Medieval Sourcebook of the Fordham University Centre for Medieval Studies.

13th century

War horse	30 pounds
Riding horse	10 pounds
Craftsman's tabard and tunic	3 shillings

14th century

Wine, best Gascon in London	4 pence a gallon
Wine, best Rhenish in London	8 pence a gallon
Ale, good	1.5 pence a gallon
Ale, medium	1 penny a gallon
Ale, poor	0.75 pence a gallon
University, student of good birth	4-10 pounds a year
Cheap sword (peasant's)	6 pence

15th century

Ready-made Milanese armour	8 pounds, 6 shillings, 8 pence
Cheap gentlewoman's funeral (bell-ringing, clergy, food)	7 pounds
Emptying of a city cesspit	6 shillings, 8 pence

16th century

Cuirass of pistol-proof with paudroons	1 pound, 6 shillings
Fencing tuition	10 shillings a month
Varnishing, replacing straps and riveting helmet and corselet	1 shilling, 4 pence
Fee for removing rust from corselets	5 pence each

Short-selling

Short-selling runs deep in financial history. Perhaps the first case dates to 1609 when the Dutch trader, Isaac Le Maire, targeted the shares of the shipping company Vereenigde Oostindische Compagnie (the Dutch East India Company). VOC was the first multinational corporation in history and had broad powers. Nonetheless, Le Maire, concerned about threats of attack by English ships, sold VOC's shares short. After learning about Le Maire's tactics, the stock exchange governing VOC's trading banned short-selling (although the ban was later revoked).

How prices change

The average prices in pence per kg (except where stated) of five essential food items at selected points since 1914.

Food item	1914	1970	1990	2004
Flour, 1.5kg	2.3	10.8	55	68
White loaf	1.2	8.8	65	91
Sugar, granulated	3	8.3	62	74
Milk	0.7	4.7	31	35
Cheddar cheese	8.4	40.8	330	567

Women on US banknotes

Martha Washington is the only woman whose portrait has appeared on a United States currency note. She appeared on the face of the $1 Silver Certificate of 1886 and 1891, and on the back of the $1 Silver Certificate of 1896.

Euro banknote production

% of production	Bank of Origin
27.1	Deutsche Bundesbank
19.0	Banque de France
16.5	Banca d'Italia
10.0	Banco de Espana
8.0	European Central Bank
5.1	De Nederlandsche Bank
3.3	Banque Nationale de Belgique
2.7	Österreichische Nationalbank
2.4	Bank of Greece
2.3	Banco de Portugal
1.6	Suomen Pankki
1.2	Central Bank of Ireland
0.4	Banka Slovenije
0.2	Central Bank of Cyprus
0.2	Banque centrae du Luxembourg
0.1	Centra Bank of Malta

Real returns

The 2007 Barclays Equity Gilt Study gave the real investment returns (%pa) of various asset classes.

Period	1996-2006	1986-2006	1956-2006	Since 1899
Equities	4.9	6.9	7.1	5.3
Gilts	4.6	5.6	2.2	1.1
Corporate bonds	6.7	-	-	-
Index-linked	4.5	4.5	-	-
Cash	2.6	3.7	2.0	1.0

A taxing war

Income tax was first implemented in the USA to help pay for the Civil War. It ran from 1861-1872 and was a tax of 3% on income in excess of $800.

Sound financial reasoning

'Money is better than poverty, if only for financial reasons.'
Woody Allen

Current account

A country's current account balance is the net value of its trades and earnings from other sources. The countries with the highest current account balances are:

Country	Balance (US$m)
China	360,700
Japan	212,800
Germany	185,000
Saudi Arabia	100,800
Russia	76,600
Switzerland	72,840
Norway	63,660
Kuwait	52,730
Netherlands	50,930
United Arab Emirates	41,670

Ten signs a company is in trouble

Robert Leach in his book *The Investor's Guide to Understanding Accounts* listed 10 signs that a company might be in trouble:

1   There are more than three photos of the chief executive in the accounts statement.

2   The accounts are difficult to find, understand or read.

3   It mentions EBITDA (earnings before tax, depreciation and amortisation).

4   The chairman's or chief executive's report mentions "difficult conditions" or "economic downturn".

5   The report also says the company is confident of meeting these challenges.

6   The accounts statement has an exceptional item for reorganisation in two consecutive years.

7   There is gearing of more than 200%.

8   There is a long explanation under "going concern" in the notes to the accounts.

9   Significant amounts are shown as exceptional items.

10   A flagpole or fountain can be seen at the company's head office.

Daily performance of UK markets

Any market trader will tell you why they don't like Mondays. This chart shows the proportion of days when the FTSE 100 index rose since 1984. Historically the UK market increases more frequently on Fridays than it does on Mondays.

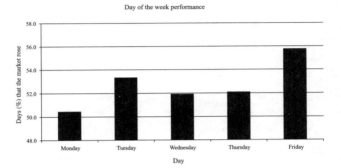

Day of the week performance

Rupee or not rupee

These countries currently have the rupee as their currency:

India, Indonesia, Maldives, Mauritius, Nepal, Pakistan, Seychelles, Sri Lanka

The rupee is an obsolete currency of these states and regions:

Afghanistan, Bhutan, Burma/Myanmar, Danish India, British East Africa, French India, German East Africa, Persian Gulf, Hyderabad, Italian Somaliland, Java, Dutch India, Portuguese India, Riau, Travancore, West Irian, Zanzibar

The Bundesländer series

In 2006 Germany began a programme to release a series of 16 coins commemorating the 16 states of the German Federal Republic. The programme will end in 2021.

The designs are as follows:

Year	State	Design
2006	Schleswig-Holstein	Holstein Gate, Lübeck
2007	Mecklenberg-Western Pomerania	Schwerin Castle
2008	Hamburg	St Michaelis' Church, Hamburg
2009	Saarland	Ludwig Church in Saarbrücken
2010	Bremen	City Hall, Bremen
2011	North Rhine Westphalia	Cologne Cathedral
2012	Bavaria	Neuschwanstein Castle, Hohenschwangau and Füssen
2013	Baden-Württemberg	Maulbronn Abbey
2014	Lower Saxony	City Hall, Hanover
2015	Hesse	City Hall, Frankfurt Am Main
2016	Saxony	Zwinger Palace, Dresden
2017	Rhineland-Palatinate	Porta Nigra Gate, Trier
2018	Berlin	Reichstag
2019	Saxony-Anhalt	Cathedral of Magdeburg
2020	Thuringia	Wartburg Castle, Eisenach
2021	Brandenburg	Sanssouci Palace, Potsdam

Zimbabwean dollar

With inflation reaching extreme levels, this is how many Z$ you would have neeeded at various points to purchase a copy of Harriman House's *Wealth of Nations*.

Date	Z$
1991	16
October 2007	16m
November 2007	24m
December 2007	64m
January 2008	96m
February 2008	320m
March 2008	1,120m
April 2008	1,600m
May 2008	12,408m
June 2008	654,848m
July 2008	12,136,480m

Hanky panky

The pocket handkerchief is by no means a prized possession in the current day, but in 18th century London a hanky was an expensive item - Charles Dickens' Artful Dodger even went to so far as to say it was his favourite object for theft. A cotton handkerchief could be resold for six pence, while a silk one might fetch six shillings, which was enough to buy a week's worth of food.

Obsolete currencies

Currency	Country or area
ackey	Gold Coast
budju	Algeria
buqsha	Yemen
escudo	Portugal
gazeta	Ionian Islands
gulden	Fribourg
hwan	South Korea
inti	Peru
karbovanets	Ukraine
livre	Guadeloupe
perper	Montenegro
piastre	Egypt
pie	India
pound	Gambia
riksdaler	Sweden
rixdollar	Ceylon
sol	Argentina
speciethaler	Schleswig-Holstein
syli	Guinea
tangka	Tibet
thaler	Danzig
tolar	Solvenia
venezolano	Venezuela

DJIA original members

The Dow Jones Industrial Average was first published in 1896 with twelve stocks listed. It is used to give an average stock value of the largest American companies. The original members were:

American Cotton Oil	American Sugar
American Tobacco	Chicago Gas
Distilling & Cattle Feeding	General Electric
Laclede Gas	National Lead
North American	Tennessee Coal & Iron
US Leather	US Rubber

Only one of these companies, General Electric, has survived in the list to the present day.

What does it cost - property?

12 bedroom, 15 bath mansion, Holmby Hills Estate, California	£83, 340, 000
8 bedroom, 10 bath house, Osprey, Florida	£12,340,000
3 bedroom house, Chelsea SW3	£1.5m - £5m
3 bedroom house, Shankhill Road, West Belfast	£125,000
4-5 berth, 60 foot narrowboat	Around £35,000
3 bedroom house, France Street, New Orleans	£33,000

Lifestyle balance sheet

'My problem lies in reconciling my gross habits with my net income.'
Errol Flynn

US government salaries

President	$400,000
Vice President	$212,100
Chief Justice, Supreme Court	$212,100
Associate Justice, Supreme Court	$203,000
Cabinet-level officials	$183,500
Speaker of the House	$165,200
Senator or Representative	$165,200

By way of contrast the average salary of a Standard & Poor's 500 listed company CEO is $11.75 million.

UK money towns

Penny Bridge, Cumbria; Pennyfuir, Argyll & Bute; Pennyghael, Argyll & Bute; Pennyglen, South Ayrshire; Pennygown, Argyll & Bute; Pennymoor, Devon; Pound Bank, Worcestershire; Pound Green, East Sussex; Pound Hill, West Sussex; Poundffald, Swansea; Poundgate, East Sussex; Poundisford Park, Somerset; Poundland, South Ayrshire; Poundon, Buckinghamshire; Poundsbridge, Kent; Poundsgate, Devon; Poundstock, Cornwall; Shillingford, Devon; Shillingford, Oxfordshire; Shillingstone, Dorset

Formula of mass destruction

The Black-Scholes formula is one of the most famous in finance. First published in 1973, it provides a mathematical model for pricing options. The model has been much criticised, traders claim not to use it, and yet its influence remains strong.

*

Financial panics have become almost commonplace; events that are meant to occur once in a millennium now seem to occur every few years. Could this be because the financial system was built on an idea [Black-Scholes model] that badly underestimates the risk of catastrophes and so conspires with human nature to create them?

*

Formula for pricing a European call option:

$$C = SN(d_1) - Ke^{-rT}N(d_2)$$

$$d_1 = (\ln(S/K) + (Y + \tfrac{1}{2}\sigma^2)T) \div \sigma\sqrt{T}$$

$$d_2 = d_1 - \sigma\sqrt{T}$$

Where:
C is the price of the call option
S is the current value of the underlying asset
Y is Yield of the underlying asset. Y = r for stock, Y = 0 for futures
σ is the volatility of the underlying asset
r is the continuous compounded interest rate
T is the time until expiration
K is the strike (exercise) price
N( ) is cumulative normal distribution
ln( ) is a natural logarithm (base e)

**

Nobel Prize in Economic Science winners

2008	Paul Krugman
2007	Leonid Hurwicz, Eric S. Maskin, Roger B. Myerson
2006	Edmund S. Phelps
2005	Robert J. Aumann, Thomas C. Schelling
2004	Finn E. Kydland, Edward C. Prescott
2003	Robert F. Engle III, Clive W.J. Granger
2002	Daniel Kahneman, Vernon L. Smith
2001	George A. Akerlof, A. Michael Spence, Joseph E. Stiglitz
2000	James J. Heckman, Daniel L. McFadden
1999	Robert A. Mundell
1998	Amartya Sen
1997	Robert C. Merton, Myron S. Scholes
1996	James A. Mirrlees, William Vickrey
1995	Robert E. Lucas Jr.
1994	John C. Harsanyi, John F. Nash Jr., Reinhard Selten
1993	Robert W. Fogel, Douglass C. North
1992	Gary S. Becker
1991	Ronald H. Coase
1990	Harry M. Markowitz, Merton H. Miller, William F. Sharpe
1989	Trygve Haavelmo
1988	Maurice Allais
1987	Robert M. Solow
1986	James M. Buchanan Jr.
1985	Franco Modigliani
1984	Richard Stone
1983	Gerard Debreu
1982	George J. Stigler
1981	James Tobin
1980	Lawrence R. Klein
1979	Theodore W. Schultz, Sir Arthur Lewis
1978	Herbert A. Simon
1977	Bertil Ohlin, James E. Meade
1976	Milton Friedman
1975	Leonid Vitaliyevich Kantorovich, Tjalling C. Koopmans
1974	Gunnar Myrdal, Friedrich August von Hayek
1973	Wassily Leontief
1972	John R. Hicks, Kenneth J. Arrow
1971	Simon Kuznets
1970	Paul A. Samuelson
1969	Ragnar Frisch, Jan Tinbergen

Top ten songs about money

1   Pet Shop Boys - Opportunities (Let's Make Lots of Money)
2   Valentine Brothers - Money's Too Tight to Mention
3   The Smiths - Money Changes Everything
4   The Beatles - Taxman
5   Madonna - Material Girl
6   The Clash - Career Opportunities
7   The Skids - Working for the Yankee Dollar
8   Abba - Money, Money, Money
9   Dire Straits - Money for Nothing
10 Pink Floyd - Money

Top ten films about trading and markets

1   Trading Places
2   Wall Street
3   The Bonfire of the Vanities
4   Rogue Trader
5   Pi
6   Boiler Room
7   Barbarians at the Gate
8   The Wheeler Dealers
9   Other People's Money
10 American Psycho

Tax resistance

In support of tax resistance:

Governments do not have a rightful claim to the fruits of people's labour, and so taxation is robbery.

Goverments may partake in activities on behalf of a state which do not correlate with the moral beliefs of the citizens of that state. Refusing to pay tax restricts funding for these activities.

Governments do not accede to power lawfully or fairly and have no right to collect taxes.

A government spends tax revenues on self-serving ends, and not for the collective good.

Large, over-reaching governments have too much influence in areas where they should not interfere.

Tax rates for the wealthy or the powerful are too low.

Governments do not spend tax revenues wisely.

Social justice is best obtained through charity and voluntary donation, not compulsory taxes.

Some take less out of the system (healthcare, education, police assistance) than others, and should pay less tax.

Non-citizens should not pay tax without first having a representative to speak for them in the government.

*

Against tax resistance:

In a constitutional democracy everyone has to obey all laws equally. By living in a country you agree to abide by its laws, tax included.

continued...

Those who do not pay taxes put an extra burden on other citizens to make up the shortfall, which is unfair.

Those who do not pay taxes enjoy the advantages of a state's infrastructure, and defence against foreign attack, without helping to pay the bill for these services.

Some argue tax resistance is ineffective, as large proportions of people in the UK and USA are already legally exempt from income tax. It is improbable that enough tax payers will be mobilised in support of a cause to actually make a significant protest.

Governments are able to levy fines, penalties and interest payments against tax evaders and will get their money eventually.

**

The price of light

Yale University research indicates a strange phenomenon with the price of light. William Nordhaus conducted some illuminating research on this subject and discovered that from its level of 40 cents per 1,000 lumen hours in 1800, the price of light has fallen to a tenth of a cent per 1,000 lumen hours today, which is a decline of 99%.

Conversely, the price of light bulbs is recorded as having increased 180% in the same period because of rises in the price of bulbs and fixtures. This means that if the price of light is taken to be just the price of the objects needed to turn electricity into light then light will seem more expensive than it is and a false impression is given. Therefore, in the area of light, inflation appears to be at a higher level than it actually is.

Deceased banks

They're stiff, bereft of life, they rest in peace! They're pushing up the daisies! They're off the twig! They've kicked the bucket, shuffled off their mortal coil and joined the choir invisible!

ABN AMRO	ARC Securities
Lehman Brothers	Albert E Sharp
Alex Brown & Co	Smith Barney
Midland Bank	Tokai Bank
Bank of Tokyo	Bankers Trust
Savory Milln	Rudolf Wolff & Co
Barings Bank	Bear Stearns

Butler Til	Capel Cure Myers	PaineWebber
Carlyle Capital	Caspian Securities	Charterhouse Tilne
Credit Lyonnais	Orion Bank	Crocker Bank
First Interstate Bank	Darier Hentsch & Cie	Dean Witter
Dillon Read	Penney Easton	EF Hutton
Enskilda Securities	Eurobrokers	First Boston
Wood Mackenzie	Texas Commerce	Vivian Gray

First National Bank of Chicago	First National Finance
First Union	FleetBoston
Fuji Bank	Shearson & Co
Giles & Cresswell	Global Trust Bank
Guinness Mahon	Hambrecht & Quist
Hambros	Harlow Butler
Refco	Hill Samuel
Kidder Peabody	L. Messel
Laurie Millbank	Liberty Eurasia
Loeb Rhodes	Lombard Odier
Mitsubishi Bank	Phillips & Drew
Orion Bank	Rowe & Pitman

Golden facts

It costs $428 to mine an ounce of gold.

*

Alchemy is theoretically possible using a nuclear reaction, but for the average person it is not practical to turn base metals into gold.

*

70% of the world's gold is used in jewellery.

*

Gold is 20 times heavier than the equivalent volume of water.

*

The word carat, for measuring the proportion of gold in jewellery, comes from carab seed. The carab seed was used in oriental markets as a scale balance.

*

Gold's chemical symbol is Au, which is derived from the latin *aurum*, meaning "glowing dawn".

*

If one ounce of gold was shaped into a thin wire it could stretch 40 miles.

*

All the gold ever mined would fit inside 64 London buses.

*

Gold is so inert that it reacts with effectively nothing, including the human body. For this reason it is safely used as a food - in gold leaf - and in alcholic drinks called *goldwasser*, produced in Eastern Europe.
15% of annual gold consumption is recycled from previously used gold.

*

A standard 6 person tablecloth is 2 metres^2 in area. Gold is so malleable that one ounce of it could be made into *eight* of these tablecloths.

**

The feel of notes

Bank of England banknotes do not have braille on them,
but there are textured areas in the following shapes on
notes to help blind people distinguish them:

£5	a circle
£10	a diamond
old £20	a square
new £20	a prominent numeral
£50	a triangle

And of course the notes are all different sizes.

What does it cost - miscellaneous?

Shakespeare Xcede 10 foot fishing rod	£30
Riley Aristocrat full size snooker table	£7,000
Pittsburgh Pirates baseball team, PNC Park 2009 season ticket, baseline	£1,242, or £15.30 a game
Chelsea Football Club, Stamford Bridge 2008 season ticket, upper west stand	£1,150, or £60.53 a game
1,000 Rexel 56 staples, 6mm	£4.60
Gentleman's top hat	£50
Two kitchen taps	£15
20 assorted tulips	£23
Box of 300 lotus biscuits	£9, or 3p a biscuit
Elton John concert ticket, Birmingham	£80
Elton John album, *Songs From The West Coast,* from a second-hand Internet shop	1p

Shares, interest rates, sterling and gold

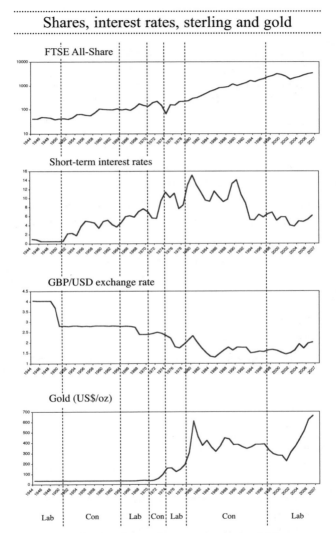

Con and Lab refer to the conservative and labour
governments in power in the respective periods.

Efficient Market Hypothesis

The efficient market hypothesis (EMH) holds that prices of traded assets reflect all known information. A corollary of the EMH is that no information or analysis will allow a trader to outperform the market.

*

The EMH has three forms:

Weak form: traded prices fully reflect all past market prices (ie, technical analysis doesn't work).

Semi-strong form: traded prices fully reflect all publicly available information (ie, fundamental analysis doesn't work).

Strong form: traded prices fully reflect all information (ie, even insider trading does not work).

*

But, before adopting the EMH as your guiding force, bear in mind these critical words from Warren Buffett:

'I'd be a bum on the street with a tin cup if the markets were always efficient.'

**

Plastic card fraud in the US

The Secret Service investigates card fraud in America, but they do not open up a new investigation unless more than $150,000 of crime has been committed. Many fraudsters are aware of this fact, and deliberately keep thefts from each business or area below this figure.

Notable financial upheavals

Tulip mania	1620s-30s
South Sea Bubble	1710s
Panic of 1837	1837
Railway mania	1840s
Long Depression	1873-96
Post-WWI hyperinflation	1918
Wall Street Crash	1929
Great Depression	1930s
Oil Shock	1973
Energy crisis	1979
Savings and Loan Crisis	1980s
Black Monday	1987
Asian financial crisis	1990s
Dot-com bubble	1995-2001
Stock market downturn	2002
United States housing bubble	2001-2007

Euro design

The euro symbol was designed by a
Belgian, Alain Billiet.

Derivative acronyms

ASTROS	Asset Return Obligation Securities
BOXES	Basket Opportunity Exchangeable Securities
CUBS	Customized Upside Basket Securities
ELKS	Enhanced Equity-Linked Debt Securities
EPICS	Exchange Preferred Income Cumulative Shares
HITS	Hybrid Income Securities Units
MITTS	Market Index Target Term Securities
PIES	Premium Income Equity Securities
QUIPS	Quarterly Income Preferred Securities
RANGERS	Risk Adjusting Equity Range Securities
SAILS	Stock Appreciation Income-Linked Securities
SATURNS	Structured Asset Trust Unit Repackaging
SIRENS	Step-Up Increasing Redeemable Equity Notes
SQUIDS	Senior Quarterly Income Debt Securities
TARGETS	Targeted Growth Enhanced Terms Securities
TIMES	Trust Issued Mandatory Exchange Securities
TRIGGERS	Target Return Investment Growth Securities
WIRES	Warrants & Income Redeemable Equity Securities
YES	Yield Enhanced Stock

Where is the euro legal tender?

The euro is legal tender in the following countries, territories, overseas departments and islands:

Belgium, Ireland, Spain, Italy, Luxembourg, The Netherlands, Portugal, Finland, San Marino, Andorra, Kosovo, French Guiana, Mayotte, Saint Pierre, French Southern and Antarctic Territories, Germany, Greece, France, Cyprus, Malta, Austria, Slovenia, Monaco, Vatican City, Montenegro, Guadeloupe, Martinique, Réunion, Miquelon.

How do you spell euro?

With the introduction of Greece to the single European currency, the Greek language also joined. Whereas in the Latin alphabet Euro is spelt just so, it is Ευρω in Greek. This is now included on all banknotes

This problem expanded still further when Bulgaria qualified to join, as they use the Cyrillic alphabet. This means Euro may need be spelt a third way on notes - Евро.

Sound familiar?

'All nations with a capitalist mode of production are seized periodically by a feverish attempt to make money without the mediation of the process of production.'
Karl Marx

JAK Members Bank

The Jord Arbete Kapital (JAK) Bank is a Swedish institution which does not pay or charge interest on loans, and whose operations are financed by member savings.

*

Points are awarded to customers who accumulate savings with JAK, and future loans are awarded based on these points. The more you save, the more you are later entitled to borrow.

*

JAK's broad guiding principles are:

Interest has a negative effect on society and environment.

*

Members are liberated economically because interest free credit is available.

*

A stable and lasting world economy can be created by having balanced rules for everyone.

**

Banana Money

When Japan occupied Singapore, Malaya, North Borneo and Sarawak and Brunei during the Second World War it issued a currency which depicted bananas on the ten dollar notes. This currency had widespread use in these occupied areas as traditional currency became scarce.

World's smallest banknote

Morocco released a 50 centimes note into circulation in 1944. It measured only 41mm x 32mm and is the world's smallest banknote.

And here is the size of the note.

Rates of passage

Here are the rates for passage to New York, Boston and Philadelphia from Liverpool on emigrant ships in 1847:

Adult	From 3 pounds, 15 shillings to 4 pounds
Child	From 2 pounds, 10 shillings to 2 pounds, 15 shillings

It is interesting to note that if children were "numerous" then they would have to pay an adult's fare because a ship could only carry 2 passengers for every 5 tons of its registered burden.

90lb coins

The largest coins ever used in the world were used in Alaska in the 19th century and were made of copper. They were a metre long, 50cm wide and weighed 40kg.

Currency symbols from around the world

฿	Thai baht
₵	Ghanaian cedi
₡	Colón sign (Costa Rica and El Salvador)
ƒ	Aruban Florin
₦	Nigerian naira
₱	Philippine peso
Sk	Slovak koruna
Rp	rupiah sign in Indonesia
＼	rupee mark (Bengal)
৳	rupee sign (Bengal)
R$	Brazilian real
S/.	Peruvian sol
₮	Mongolian tögrög
₩	Korean won
¥	Chinese Renminbi yuan/Japanese yen
zł	Polish Złoty
₴	Ukrainian hryvnia
₪	Israeli sheqel
៛	Cambodian riel
ﺭﯾﺎﻝ	Iranian Rial
руб	Russian ruble

£5 through time

This table shows the value of money that would be
needed in 2007 to buy the value of goods £5 would have
purchased in the following year.

Year	2007 equivalent
1850	£412
1860	£339
1870	£343
1880	£357
1890	£394
1900	£388
1910	£366
1920	£144
1930	£227
1940	£196
1950	£123
1960	£83
1970	£56
1980	£15
1990	£8
2000	£6

Das Kapital

*'I wish that dear Karl could have spent more time
acquiring capital instead of merely writing about it.'*
Jenny Marx

Types of yield curve

The yield curve illustrates the range of interest rates for different maturities (usually ranging from overnight to 30-year bond rates). The shape of the yield curve can be interpreted as meaning:

Normal yield curve This curve will show a positive incline, in line with the anticipation of future economic growth and rising inflation. Of course, in a period of persistent deflation the curve will be negative.

*

Steep yield curve A steep yield will be apparent as economic expansion begins, or as a period of recession comes to an end. The depressed interest rates that come with economic slowdown will be replaced with rising rates.

*

Flat or humped yield curve A level curve occurs when all securities mature with similar yields. This gives the indication of doubts about the economy. With a humped curve short and long-term yields mature with the same value, while medium-term yields are higher.

*

Inverted yield curve This provides reliable evidence for a declining economic situation. It occurs when long-term yields are lower than short-term yields, and indicates recession 12-18 months in advance.

**

Money market yield curve

A list of standard instruments used to build a money market yield curve.

Type	Settlement date
Cash	Overnight rate
Cash	Tomorrow next rate
Cash	1m
Cash	3m
Future	Nearest month*
Future	2nd nearest month*
Future	3rd nearest month*
Future	4th nearest month*
Future	5th nearest month*
Swap	2y
Swap	3y
Swap	4y
Swap	5y
Swap	7y
Swap	10y
Swap	15y
Swap	20y
Swap	30y

*On the quarterly futures contract cycle.

Pioneers of finance

Date	Pioneer	Research area
1900	Louis Bachelier	Discovered that stock price changes are unpredictable.
1930s	Benjamin Graham	Published the classic work *Security Analysis*, and advocated the value style of investing.
1952	Harry Markowitz	Studied the relationship between risk and return for investors.
1958	James Tobin	"Market portfolios" - a method for investors to maximise their return relative to the risk incurred.
1958	Franco Modigliani/Merton Miller	Conducted research into capital structure.
1964	William F. Sharpe	Developed the Beta and Capital Asset Pricing Model.
1965	Eugene Fama	Produced the (now controversial) efficient market hypothesis.
1973	Myron Scholes and Fischer Black	Black and Scholes option pricing model.
1977	Sanjoy Basu	Found that an anomoly to the EMH is a stock's P/E ratio.
1980s and 1990s	Amos Tversky Daniel Kahneman Richard Thaler	Behavioural finance - studying investors' behavioural patterns.

Interesting counter-arguments

Interest has not always been accepted as a good thing.

In the **Middle Ages** time was regarded as God's property, and it was sinful to make money - through interest - with God's property.

*

Also in the **Middle Ages** a loan was bequeathed usually out of necessity on behalf of the debtor (because of drought or disease) and as such to charge interest was unreasonable.

*

Thomas Aquinas believed that to demand interest payments was to ask a buyer to pay for something twice, and was unjust.

*

The **Second Lateran Council of the Catholic Church** viewed the settling of debts with more than the sum loaned as usury.

*

Islamic Sharia Law shares this view that the charging of interest is usurous, and Islamic banks are founded on this basis.

*

The Swedish **JAK bank** neither pays nor charges interest on investments and loans.

**

Stock market adages

The trend is your friend

Sell in May and go away

Buy on the rumour and sell on the news

Never try to catch a falling knife

Buy low, sell high

Buy on the dips

Don't marry your stocks

Nobody rings a bell at the market bottom

The market hates uncertainty

A rising tide lifts all boats

As goes January, so goes the year

Buy into weakness

Don't fight the Fed

Don't fight the tape

If you're going to panic, panic early

Cash is king

If Santa Claus should fail to call, bears may come to Broad & Wall

Never sell a dull market short

Sell into any rally

Sell into strength

Sell to the sleeping point

When the tiger is away, the monkeys rule the jungle

Fictional currencies

Star Wars	Galactic credit standard
Harry Potter	Galleons, sickles and knuts
Zelda, Land of Hyrule	Rupees
Lord of the Rings, Gondor	Copper, bronze, silver, gold and mithrill coins
The Flintstones, Bedrock	Clams
Final Fantasy	Gil
Startrek Voyager	Replicator rations
Doctor Who	Nargs
Judge Dredd	Creds
Scrooge McDuck universe	Number one dime
Red Dwarf	Dollarpounds and pennycents
Street Fighter	Bison dollars
Hitchhiker's Guide To The Galaxy	Altairian dollars
SimCity, The Sims, The Urbz	Simoleon
Cowboy Bebop	Woolong
Discworld, Ankh-Morpork	Ankh-Morpork dollars

Quick money

The figures in this table illustrate how many minutes it took ten companies to earn $1,000,000 of revenue and £1,000,000 of profit in 2007 (assuming they worked constantly).

Company	Minutes taken to turnover US$1m	Minutes needed to earn US$1m of profit (or losses)
Wal-Mart Stores	1.4	41.3
Exxon Mobil	1.4	12.9
Royal Dutch Shell	1.5	16.8
BP	1.8	25.2
Toyota Motor	2.3	34.9
Chevron	2.5	28.1
ING Group	2.6	41.6
Total	2.8	29.1
General Motors	2.9	(13.6)
ConocoPhillips	2.9	44.2

For purposes of comparison, taking the average American salary to be $35,000 a year, a normal working person would need 16,425,000 minutes (or 28.5 years), without spending any money, to accumulate $1,000,000.

Odd financial terms and names

Amortisation is the depreciation in value of assets or amounts, for example the amortisation of a debt by making regular payments, or the amortisation of a patent's value over time.

Beta measure the relative volatility of a share. A stock or share with a beta value of more than 1 is volatile relative to other shares in the index. A stock with a beta of less than 1 is thought to be stable.

CAT is a short notation for a catastrophe bond. Insurance companies issue these bonds in the event of a "catastrophe" which leaves them having to pay out on a number of policies.

Churning refers to the practice of over-trading the assets of a portfolio (sometimes with a view to generating extra commission).

Dead cat bounce describes a temporary recovery in a stock market following a sharp period of decline.

Gilt denotes a bond sold by the government. They are gilt-edged, and risk-free, bonds because when they mature the government, at very least, can print money to pay them off.

Junk bond is a bond with much greater risk than a government bond. They offer high interest rates for a high risk investment.

Stagging is the term given to the act of buying a share at its initial public offering price and selling it on immediately for a profit. This is also called flipping.

The fortune line

This chart shows the FT All Share index performance since 1946.

The straight line is a line of best fit calculated with regression analysis.

*

The equation of the line of best fit is $y = 24.668e^{0.0067x}$

If one believes that the long-term trend of the stock market since 1946 will continue the equation can be used to forecast future values of the FT All Share Index. For example, the equation forecasts that the Index will have a value of 12,044 in December 2022.

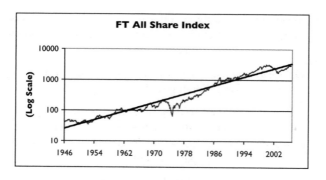

Formula for happiness and misery

Annual income twenty pounds, annual expenditure nineteen nineteen six, *result* = happiness.

Annual income twenty pounds, annual expenditure twenty pounds ought and six, *result* = misery.

Wilkins Micawber, in Charles Dickens' *David Copperfield*

Big Mac Index

The Economist has devised a method to indicate how overvalued or undervalued currencies around the world are. Their Big Mac Index compares the cost of a Big Mac in different countries. According to their Big Mac Index, in 2008:

Five most overvalued currencies:

Currency	Over-valuation
Norwegian krone	121%
Swedish krona	79%
Swiss franc	78%
Danish krone	67%
Euro	50%

Five most undervalued currencies:

Currency	Under-valuation
Malaysia ringgit	- 52%
Hong Kong dollar	- 52%
Chinese yuan	- 49%
Thai baht	- 48%
Indonesian rupiah	- 43%

Happiness is a full wallet

'What's the use of happiness? It can't buy you money.'
Henry Youngman

IMF

The International Monetary Fund was conceived at a conference in New Hampshire in 1944. The governments represented at the conference agreed to enter into a new era of international economic cooperation in an effort to prevent such occurences as the depression of the 1930s. On the whole the role of the IMF is to stabilise international financial and monetary conditions, and reduce poverty. It does this by monitoring those countries whose economies directly affect the international economic balance. If necessary the IMF can lend money to governments, or offer them advice, to help prevent financial crises.

Another large part of the IMF's work is promoting the development of poorer countries by offering loans and technical training on how to improve and manage financial institutions.

*

Membership: 185 countries

Members with low incomes: 78

Staff of the IMF: 2,600

Loans outstanding: US$19.4bn

**

Newton's mint

Sir Isaac Newton was Master of the Royal Mint from 1699 to 1727.

Special Drawing right (SDR)

The SDR is a basket currency established by the IMF for accounting purposes, and to assist with international exchange.

The value of the SDR is determined by taking the sum of the values of the four currencies in the basket, in US$. The current four members are the euro, the US dollar, the British pound and the Japanese yen. These currencies, and their weightings within the basket, are reviewed every five years.

*

Weightings for 2006-2010

Yen	11%
Euro	34%
Pound	11%
Dollar	44%

*

The SDR is calculated each day to take account of fluctuations in exchange rates. The current value of SDR1 is approximately US$1.6.

**

Cash is not everything

There is no federal statute in the United States which mandates that private businesses must accept cash as a form of payment.

Hi Ho silver

Silver is mentioned in the Bible, in the book of Genesis.

*

On a 25th wedding anniversary you should give your spouse silver.

*

Silver is the best conducter of heat and electricity of all the metal elements.

*

Silver was first coined for use as money by the Lydians - whose kingdom was situated in modern day Turkey - in the eighth century BC.

*

In more than ten languages the words for silver and money are the same.

*

The latin for silver is argentum, which is where Argentina derives its name from. This is also the reason why silver's chemical symbol is Ag.

*

Jack Kirby created the comic book character Silver Surfer in the 1960s. His hovering surfboard can travel faster than the speed of light.

*

In the UK the word "pound" is derived from the time when the value of one pound represented one troy pound of sterling silver.

*

To be born with a silver spoon in your mouth is a dual benefit: obviously you have rich parents because silver is expensive, but it also has purifying and bactericidal properties, so you will remain healthy.

**

Money slang

pony, long one, squid, century, brown, French loaf,
coppers, carpet, brass, buck, monkey, moola, jack,
macaroni, quid, skrilla, Bernie, dough, Tom mix, flag,
wonga, deep sea diver, quarter, plaster, handful, doonup,
kybosh, bullet, coal, thick one, sprat, caser, hog,
bullseye, net gen, lettuce, Hampden roar, simoleon,
rocket, iron man, sinker, dibs, bar, pap, Bobby Moore,
greens, shrapnel, fish, folding green, clam, exis, yard,
nugget, mother hen, deener, tilbury, roll, dosh, boodle,
edge pence, Lady Godiva, plenty, sheets, grand, lizard,
quap, wagon wheel, Tony Benn, poppy, deaner, half a
bar, wad, Sprarsy Anna, tosheroon, fiver, Joes, pair of
knickers, bluey, bacon, tenner, spondulicks, pieces,
huckleberry hound, marigold, readies, coconut, roffe,
rock, browny, wedge, doubloons, Pavarotti, Benjamin,
two-bit, Alan Wicker, stretch, trey, Pam Shriver, a big
one, archer, loonie, bean, boffo, wicker basket, cherry,
oxford, motsa, C-note, drinking voucher, smacker,
cabbage, in the green, bread and honey, frogskin, Elsie,
Maggie, plug, rhino, potatoes, Aryton Senna, large,
dime, sourdough, string of ponies, Sir Isaac, nicker,
score, ewif gens, fin, one-er, long green, dirty, zack,
yellowback, McGarret, garden gate, heptagonal bad boy,
lolly, oscar, joey, K, bag of sand, ned, strike, farthing,
flag, gen, gorilla, dinarly, clod, Jack's alive, G, ace,
bone, cock and hen, point, simon, mill, commodore, ton,
daddler, taxi driver, green back, bob, bottle, doughnut,
bar, Nelson Eddys, bender, chump change, kick, dosh,
beer tokens, flimsy, beehive, deuce, bice, tanner, poorly
fish, rivets, spanner, Rio, Desmond Tutu, big ben, thrifty,
cows, biscuit, chip, job

Euro mint marks

On euro coins mint marks are used to identify the
country where they were minted.

Country	Symbol	City of Mint
Belgium		Brussels
Finland		Helsinki-Vantaa
France		Pessac
Germany	A D F G J	Berlin Munich Stuttgart Karlsruhe Hamburg
Greece		Athens
Italy	R	Rome
Luxembourg (2002-04)		Utrecht
Luxembourg (2005-06)		Helsinki-Vantaa

continued...

Country	Symbol	City of Mint
Luxembourg (2007-)		Pessac
Monaco		Pessac
Netherlands		Utrecht
Poland		Warsaw
Portugal	INCM (Imprensa National-Casa de Moeda)	Lisbon
San Marino	R	Rome
Slovakia	MK	Kremnica
Slovenia (2007)	Fi	Helsinki-Vantaa
Spain		Madrid

The state of quarters today

In 1999 President Clinton authorised The 50 State Quarters Programme which commemorates each state with a unique design on a 25 cent coin.

The eagle will retake its spot on the quarter when the programme ends in 2008.

Year	State	Design
1999	Delaware	Caesar Rodney on horseback
	Pennsylvania	Commonwealth statue
	New Jersey	George Washington crossing Delaware River
	Georgia	Peach and oak sprigs
	Connecticut	Charter oak
2000	Masschusetts	Minuteman statue
	Maryland	State house
	South Carolina	Palmetto tree, Carolina wren
	New Hampshire	Old man of the mountain
	Virginia	Susan Constant, Godspeed, Discovery
2001	New York	Statue of Liberty, eleven stars
	North Carolina	Wright flyer
	Rhode Island	America's Cup yacht
	Vermont	Maple trees
	Kentucky	Racehorse, Bardstown mansion
2002	Tennessee	Fiddle, trumpet, guitar, three stars
	Ohio	Wright flyer, astronaut
	Louisiana	Pelican, trumpet
	Indiana	Racing car, 19 stars
	Mississippi	Magnolia blossoms

Year	State	Design
2003	Illinois	Abraham Lincoln, Chicago, 21 stars
	Alabama	Helen Keller, pine branch, magnolia
	Maine	Permaquid Point lighthouse
	Missouri	Gateway Arch, Lewis and Clark
	Arkansas	Diamond, rice, a mallard duck
2004	Michigan	Outline of great lakes
	Florida	Spanish galleon, sabal trees, space shuttle
	Texas	Rope, five pointed star
	Iowa	Schoolhouse, a tree being planted
	Wisconsin	Cows, cheese, corn
2005	California	John Muir, condor, Half Dome, sequoia
	Minnesota	Fishing
	Oregon	Crater Lake National Park
	Kansas	Bison, sunflowers
	West Virginia	New River gorge bridge
2006	Nevada	Mustangs, mountains, sun, sagebrush
	Nebraska	Chimney Rock, wagon
	Colorado	Longs Peak
	North Dakota	Bison, badlands
	South Dakota	Mount Rushmore, pheasant, wheat
2007	Montana	Bison skull, Missouri River
	Washington	Salmon, Mount Rainier
	Idaho	Peregrine falcon
	Wyoming	Bucking bronco
	Utah	Completion of the transcontinental railroad
2008	Oklahoma	Flycatcher, Indian blanket wildflower
	New Mexico	Zia sun symbol
	Arizona	Grand Canyon
	Alaska	Grizzly bear eating salmon, North Star
	Hawaii	Statue of Kamehameha I

UK chancellors

UK chancellors of the exchequer since 1945.

Hugh Dalton	1945-47
Stafford Cripps	1947-50
Hugh Gaitskell	1950-51
Rab Butler	1951-55
Harold Macmillan	1955-57
Peter Thorneycroft	1957-58
Derick Heathcoat Amory	1958-60
Selwyn Lloyd	1960-62
Reginald Maudling	1962-64
James Callaghan	1964-67
Roy Jenkins	1967-70
Iain Macleod	1970
Anthony Barber	1970-74
Denis Healey	1974-79
Geoffrey Howe	1979-83
John Major	1989-90
Norman Lamont	1990-93
Kenneth Clarke	1993-97
Gordon Brown	1997-2007
Alistair Darling	2007-present

Fixed exchange rates of pre-euro currencies

Exchange for € 1	Currency
1,936.27	Italian lira
340.75	Greek drachma
239.64	Slovenian tolar
200.48	Portugese escudu
166.39	Spanish pesesta
40.34	Belgian franc
40.34	Luxembourg franc
14.76	Austrian schilling
6.56	French franc
5.95	Finnish mark
2.20	Dutch guilder
1.95	Deutsche mark
0.79	Irish pound
0.59	Cypriot pound
0.43	Maltese lira

Origins of the London Stock Exchange

The LSE itself was founded in 1801, but there is evidence of a trade in securities in the 17th century. It was in 1698 that John Castaing began to issue a list of stock and commodity prices called "The Course of the Exchange and Other Things" from his London office (in Jonathan's Coffee House).

Tax freedom day

Tax is usually paid each month as a deduction from income. But imagine if the government took all of your income each month from the beginning of the year until your annual tax bill had been paid.

*

With this in mind, each year the Adam Smith Institute calculates the average date at which most UK residents would have finished paying tax and could begin working for themselves. This date is called *tax freedom day*. The earliest date it has fallen on was 23 April in 1964, but for 2006 the date was 3 June.

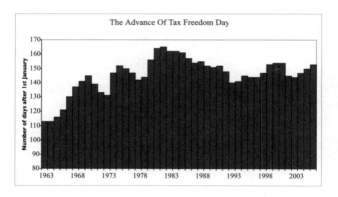

The selfish butcher

'It is not from the benevolence of the butcher, the brewer, or the baker, that we expect our dinner, but from their regard to their own interest.'
Adam Smith, *Wealth of Nations*

Security features of euro banknotes

There are allegedly many undisclosed security features of euro banknotes, but some which are known follow:

The notes are not completely flat, but have some areas of raised text.

*

On the front, right side of the notes there is a denominational hologram.

*

Some notes feature areas printed with magnetic ink.

*

Adding up the numbers in the serial code produces the number 8. For example, if the serial code was A12463, complete the calculation (replacing A with its position in the alphabet):

$$1 + 1 + 2 + 4 + 6 + 3 = 17$$

$$1 + 7 = 8$$

You have a genuine note.

*

Each denomination of note has a special watermark printed into the paper.

*

A barcode is printed next to the watermark, which can be scanned to reveal the denomination.

*

There are textured lines on the notes which are made of of the word Euro in very small print.

*

Infrared and ultraviolet watermarks - special watermarks that can be seen in the right light.

**

Taxes on the poorest 30%

Countries where the poorest 30% of the population contribute the most to the total tax budget.

Country	Proportion paid (%)
Denmark	14
Netherlands	12
Sweden	11
Norway	10
Germany	10
Finland	10
France	9
Italy	7
USA	6
Canada	6

Taxes on the richest 30%

Countries where the richest 30% of the population contribute the most to the total tax budget.

Country	Proportion paid (%)
France	68
Ireland	66
USA	65
Australia	65
Belgium	64
Italy	62
UK	62
Canada	60
Finland	57
Norway	54

Monarchs on UK banknotes

George II was the first British monarch to have his portrait on UK banknotes. He, along with George III and George IV, appeared on Royal Bank of Scotland notes. George V has also featured, appearing on the 10 shilling and 1 pound notes issued by the British Treasury between 1914 and 1928.

1929 recovery

After the 1929 crash, the Dow Jones Industrial Average did not recover its pre-cash level until 1954 - a full 25 years later.

Buying bread

The countries where people work longest to earn enough to buy a loaf of bread.

Country	Time (mins)
Japan	15
United States	14
Austria	13
Italy	12
France	11
Ireland	11
Belgium	9
Finland	8
New Zealand	8
Norway	8

Income received by the richest 10%

Countries where income is most heavily distributed towards the richest 10%.

Portion of country's income (%)	Country
50	Swaziland
49	Nicaragua
48	Brazil
48	Central African Republic
47	Burkino Faso
46	Columbia
46	Guatemala
46	South Africa
46	Chile
44	Paraguay

Imports from USA

US$m	Country
41,164	Canada
22,702	Mexico
12,547	Japan
8,717	UK
7,382	Germany
6,466	China
6,050	South Korea
4,924	Netherlands
4,406	France
4,060	Singapore

Origin of dividends

The first companies to pay dividends were overseas trading companies in the 17th century, such as the Dutch East India Company. They paid dividends varying between 12-25% each year. Shareholders did not always receive their dividends in cash though: payments were also made with bonds or in kind (with spices). Shareholders were known as the "pepper sacks of Amsterdam" for this reason.

Cost of mail

In the late 18th and early 19th centuries, the UK government increased taxes on post rather than on coal. This could just about be justified during the wars with France when the tax was used to fund the military, but when hostilities ended in 1815 people became unhappy with the high price of posting a letter. For example, for an ordinary working man it would cost as much as a day's wages to receive a letter.

The receiver of a letter customarily paid the postage costs, and so one method to get around paying for a letter was to put an empty envelope in the post to a friend or family member. The handwriting of the address on the envelope would identify to the receiver that the sender was alive and well - they could then refuse to accept the letter, saying they did not know who it was from, and thus avoid paying for it.

Liberty

'There can be no liberty unless there is economic liberty.'
Margaret Thatcher

Candlestick cheat sheet

Japanese candlesticks are one way of creating charts of historic prices. The candlesticks are constructed using the open, high, low and close prices of the timeframe specified. The difference between the open and close gives us the "Real Body". The extremes of the day give us the "tails" or "wicks" of the candle, known as the upper and lower shadows.

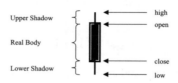

Bullish Marabuzo
Bullish: Big range day where the market opened near the low and closed near the high. The Bulls were in charge for the majority of the session.

Bearish Marabuzo
Bearish: Big range day where the market opened near the high and closed near it's lows. The Bears were in charge for the majority of the session.

Shooting Star
Bearish when seen in an uptrend. The upper shadow is at least twice the length of the real body, which is at the bottom of the day's range.

Hammer
Bullish reversal signal if it comes in a downtrend, it indicates that the market is "hammering out" a bottom. The lower shadow must be at least twice the length of the short real body – which is at the top of the candle's range.

Inverted Hammer
A Bullish pattern if seen in a downtrend. Requires confirmation as it's not generally the strongest of signals.

Hanging Man
The same shape as a Hammer but Bearish in an Uptrend. This also needs further confirmation.

Doji
Indecision: The open and close at the same level proves that buyers and sellers are balancing each other out. Signals a reversal if seen in a solid up or down trend.

Harami
A small real body contained within the previous day's real body signals a reversal if the first real body is in line with the underlying trend. Shown is a Bullish Harami. Not a strong signal.

Bullish Engulfing Pattern
Bullish if seen during a downtrend. The second open/white candle must totally envelop the real body of the first.

Bearish Engulfing Pattern
Bearish when you're in an Uptrend. The real body of the second filled/dark candle engulfs the real body of the first. A strong reversal signal especially if there is better volume on the second day.

Piercing Pattern
Bullish if seen during a downtrend. Gaps lower on the second day, then rallies strongly into the close. Has to close above the first candle's real body midpoint.

Dark Cloud Cover
Bearish if seen during an uptrend. Gaps higher on the second day, then sells off heavily into the close. Has to close below the first candle's real body midpoint.

Morning Star
A significant reversal if seen in a downtrend. It has three candles, the first two are a "Star", the third confirms, closing well into the real body of the first candle.

Evening Star
An important Bearish Pattern if seen in an uptrend. The middle candle has a small real body which gaps way from the first. The third candle confirms the change of sentiment.

History of the *Financial Times*

1884   The *Financial News* established by Harry Marks.

1888   The *Financial Times* launched as "the friend of the Honest Financier and the Respectable Broker".

1893   The *FT* is first printed on pink paper.

1919   Berry Bros, owners of *The Sunday Times* and later the *Daily Telegraph*, take control of the *FT*.

1935   30-share index introduced in *Financial Times*.

1945   Brendan Bracken buys *FT*, merges with *Financial News* but keeps pink paper and *Financial Times* name.

1945   Lex column introduced.

1953   "Industry" "Commerce" and "Public Affairs" introduced to masthead, reflecting increased scope of the newspaper.

1957   *FT* taken over by Pearson.

1961   Average circulation exceeds 132,000.

1985   *FT* starts printing in New York.

1986   Circulation passes 250,000 mark on back of "No *FT*, No Comment" campaign.

1989   Relocation of FT Group Head Office from Bracken House to Number One Southwark Bridge.

1994   First edition of "How To Spend It" magazine published.

1997   Launch of the US edition.

1998   International circulation sales overtake UK circulation sales.

2001   *FT* circulation hits 500,000.

Commemorative 50p coin designs

Year	Design	Commemorates
1973	Nine clasped hands	UK joining the EEC
1992-3	Table with seats and stars	Britain's presidency of the EC
1994	Ships and planes invading	50 years since Normany landings
1998	12 stars	25 years since Britain joined the EU
1998	Hands holding rays of the sun	50 years of the NHS
2000	Open book and a library	150 years since the Public Libraries Act
2003	A suffragette	100 years since the formation of the Women's Social and Political Union
2004	A runner's legs and a stopwatch	50 years since Roger Bannister ran a mile in under 240 seconds
2005	Definitions of "fifty" and "pence"	250 years since Samuel Johnson's *Dictionary of the English Language* was published
2006	Victoria Cross, or a soldier carrying a wounded colleague	150 years of the Victoria Cross
2007	Fleur-de-lys	100 years of scouting

Commemorative £2 coin design

Year	Design	Commemorates
1986	Thistle and St Andrew's Cross	Scottish Commonwealth Games
1989	W and M, for William and Mary	300 years since the English Bill of Rights
1994	Bank of England seal	300 years of the Bank of England
1995	Dove carrying live branch	50 years since the end of the WWII
1995	Flags and UN symbol	50 years of the UN
1996	A football	European Championships of Football, held in England
1999	A rugby stadium, rugby ball and goal posts	Rugby World Cup
2001	An imagining of Marconi's wireless tansmission	100 years since the transmission
2002	Athelete with banner, St George's flag	Commonwealth Games, Manchester
2003	DNA double helix	50 years since DNA's structure was discovered
2004	Richard Trevithick's locomotive	200 years since Trevithick's locomotive was built
2005	Parliamentary maces, episcopal crooks and swords	400 years since the gunpowder plot
2005	St Paul's Cathedral and searchlights	60 years since the end of the Second World War
2006	Roof of Paddington Station Brunel's portrait, Royal Albert Bridge	200 years since Isambard Kingdom Brunel's birth
2007	Broken chain	200 years since the slave trade was abolished
2007	Jigsaw - the piecing together of Scottish thistle and English rose	300 years since the Acts of Union
2008	Running track	100 years since the London Olympics of 1908

Commemorative £5 coin designs

Year	Design	Commemorates
1990	Crown, a cypher in a duplicate letter "E", rose and thistle	90th birthday of the Queen Mother
1993	St Edward's Crown and 40 trumpets	40 years since Queen Elizabeth II's Coronation
1996	Windsor Castle and five flags	70th birthday of Queen Elizabeth II
1997	Shield of Our Royal Arms and Shield of Prince Philip, a crown and an anchor	50th wedding anniversary of Queen Elizabeth II and Prince Philip
1998	Portrait of Prince Charles	Prince Charles' 50th birthday
1999	Portrait of Diana, Princess of Wales	In memory of Diana
1999-2000	Map of British Isles and a clock with hands set to 12 o'clock	Millenium
2000	Portrait of Queen Mother	Queen Mother's 100th birthday
2001	A "V", portrait of Queen Victoria and Crystal Palace	100 years since the death of Queen Victoria
2002	Portrait of Queen Elizabeth II	Queen's Golden Jubilee
2002	Portrait of Queen Mother and a wreath	In memory of the Queen Mother
2003	"God Save The Queen"	50 years since Queen Elizabeth II's coronation
2004	Figures of Britannia and Marianne	100 years of the Entente Cordiale between Great Britain and France
2005	HMS Victory	200 years since the Battle of Trafalgar
2005	Portrait of Horatio Nelson	200 years since Nelson's death
2006	Trumpets	Queen Elizabeth II's 80th birthday
2007	Westminster Abbey's rose window	Diamond wedding anniversary of Queen Elizabeth II and Prince Philip

How UK tax is spent

Naturally, all of the money paid to the UK government in tax is spent, but where does it go?

5% is spent on interest on government borrowings.

*

0.5% is paid to the EU as Britain's contribution to that institution.

*

27% is paid in benefits or protections for those with little or no income.

*

16% is spent on the NHS.

*

13% goes on education.

*

6% is spent on defence and the military.

*

27% is paid in wages to the public sector (though of course this also includes some of the money spent on the NHS, education and defence).

*

Finally, 1% of the tax intake is spent on collecting tax, and deciding where it should be spent.

**

Debt management

'A banker is a fellow who lends you his umbrella when the sun is shining, but wants it back the minute it begins to rain.'
Mark Twain

UK taxpayers

Of the 60 million people in Britain, 29 million people earn very little, or nothing at all:

3 million are babies

8 million are of school age

200,000 are at university

1.7 million are unemployed

74,000 are in prison

9 million are retired

A number live on the proceeds of crime

A number live from rents and inherited wealth

A number are disabled, or are fulltime mothers, fathers or carers

*

That leaves 31 million in employment, but 5 million of these work in the public sector, and so their wages are paid out of the tax budget.

*

This means that the tax paid by 26 million people has to support the full population.

*

The average tax bill for a household over a 40 year working life, and 15 years retirement, is estimated to be £600,000.

**

Ten important books about economics

In Harriman's *Politipedia* Nick Inman proposed these works as the ten most important ever written about economics.

Adam Smith	*An Inquiry into the Nature and Causes of the Wealth of Nations* (1776)
David Ricardo	*Principles of Political Economy and Taxation* (1817)
Karl Marx	*Das Kapital* (1867)
Carl Menger	*Principles of Economics* (1871)
Richard Tawney	*The Acquisitive Society* (1921)
John Maynard Keynes	*The General Theory of Employment, Interest and Money* (1936)
Friedrich Hayek	*The Road to Serfdom* (1944)
John K. Galbraith	*The Affluent Society* (1958)
Milton Friedman	*Capitalism and Freedom* (1962)
E. F. Schumacher	*Small is Beautiful: A Study of Economics As If People Mattered* (1973)

Retail price index

The retail price index (RPI) was started in the UK in June 1947. It is used to measure inflation from year to year and over the long-term. The government use the index to gauge how much they should raise pensions by, and landlords may use it to assess how much of an annual increase there should be in the rent they charge.

*

Major developments in the RPI:

1956   The index is expanded to cover all wage earning households, not just the working classes. Also at this time equivalent rents are introduced to give an indication of what rent house owners would pay if they rented. Motor vehicle purchase costs are included for the first time too.

1968   The new grouping of "Meals out" is introduced for the first time.

1975   Mortgage interest payments are included to make owner-occupiers housing costs more accurate.

1987   The structure of the index is changed, with durable household goods, miscellaneous goods and services groups being split into five new groups: household goods, leisure goods, personal goods and services, household services and leisure services.

1993   Foreign holidays are included in the leisure services group.

1994   UK holidays are included in the leisure services group.

1995   Housing depreciation is incorporated into housing costs.

Gold fixing

Gold fixing is the process by which the price of gold is set for the London market. The participants in the fixing are:

ScotiaMocatta, Barclays Capital, Deutsche Bank, HSBC, Société Générale

*

Twice each day, at 10.30 GMT and 15.00 GMT, the members of the fixing pool communicate by telephone to complete the fixing. The rate they decide upon affects the price of gold products in markets throughout the world.

*

The fixing is quite an ideosyncratic procedure. Before telephones were used the fixing took place in an office in St Swithin's Lane, London. At the fixing meetings a member could place a small Union flag on their desk to pause the process, but now that telephones are used the particpants may say "flag" to initiate a pause. If rates have been set with no objections the chair of the fixing pool says "There are no flags, and we're fixed."

*

The fixing began in 1919, and the highest level reached is $865.35 per troy ounce, at the 10.30 GMT fixing on 3 January 2008.

**

Coining offences at the Old Bailey

In the period 1686-1695 there were 400 coining offences recorded in the Proceedings records of the Old Bailey. This constituted 10% of the court's business.

Offshore financial centres

An offshore financial centre is defined as a location
which is conducive as a base for offshore companies.
Hence, these locations have low tax and/or little
regulation of business.

*

Offshore centres as classified by the IMF:

Andorra, Anguilla, Antigua, Aruba, Bahamas, Bahrain,
Barbados, Belize, Bermuda, British Virgin Islands,
Cayman Islands, Cook Islands, Costa Rica, Cyprus,
Djibouti, Dominica, Dublin, Ghana, Grenada, Guam,
Guernsey, Hong Kong, Isle of Man, Israel, Japan, Jersey,
Labuan, Lebanon, Liechtenstein, Luxembourg, Macau,
Malta, Marianas, Marshall Islands, Mauritius,
Micronesia, Montserrat, Nauru, Netherlands Antilles,
Niue, Panama, Philippines, Puerto Rico, Seychelles,
Singapore, St Kitts and Nevis, St Lucia, St Vincent and
the Grenadines, Switzerland, Tahiti, Tangier, Thailand,
Turks and Caicos, some states of the USA, Uruguay,
Vanuatu, Western Samoa

**

Caesar

*'Render unto Caesar the things which are Caesar's, and
unto God the things that are God's.'* (Matthew 22:21)

Believed to have been spoken by Jesus, it is proffered by
some Christians that this phrase justifies paying taxes
and obeying the governments on earth.

English dollars

The word "dollar" appeared in the English language long before the formation of the United States of America. The English form of the word is derived from "thaler", the name which was given to coins minted from silver in 16th century Bohemia.

Only the very first few British settlers were arriving in North America when Shakespeare wrote the following passage, found in *Macbeth*:

Act 1, Scene 2:

Rosse: That now, Sweno, the Norway's King, craves composition. Nor would we deign him burial of his men, till he disbursed at Saint Colme's Inch, ten thousand dollars to our general use.

Queen's head

Queen Elizabeth II appears on the banknotes of 34 countries.

Types of plastic card fraud

Total losses to fraud (%)	Fraud method
50	Phone/online
23	Counterfeit
16	Lost/solen
7	Card ID theft
4	Lost in the post

US stocks and bonds

In his *Four Pillars of Investing* William Bernstein presented the following table to summarise the returns and risks in US stocks and bonds in the 20th century.

Asset	Annualised Return	Worst Real Three-Year Loss
Treasury Bills	4%	0%
Treasury Bonds	5%	-25%
Large Company Stocks	10%	-60%
Small Company Stocks	12%	-70%

What are you worth?

'People's wealth and worth are very rarely related.'
Malcolm Forbes

Agorist class theory

An agorist perceives the different members of a capitalist system in interesting ways.

Entrepreneurs and venture capitalists	The foundation of the free-market - the innovators, producers and engines of progress.
Holders of capital	Not as important as the innovators. Regarded as non-thinking and ideologically lacking.
State-led capitalists	The primary evil in a market - the free-market is not able to run its course with state direction.

Economic systems

Economic systems can be roughly subdivided in terms of how much of a role the government has in running the economy:

State directed, much restriction of persons and businesses:

Marxian socialism, Socialist planned economy, Market socialism, Feudalism, Corporatism, Mercantilism

*

Community directed, much restriction of persons and business:

Anarcho-communism, Libertarian socialism, Participatory economics

*

Business directed, few restrictions on individuals and corporations:

Anarchco-capitalism, Laissez-faire capitalism, Corporate capitalism, Gift economy, Mutualism

*

Community directed, few restrictions on individuals and businesses:

Syndicalism, Mutualism, Non-property system, Libertarian socialism

*

Mixed systems:

Distributism, Georgism, Dirigisme, Nordic model, Japanese system, Mercantilism, Social market economy, Progressive utilisation theory, Indicative planning

**

How to launder money

Once you have your bulk cash proceeds they need to be placed carefully to avoid arousing suspicion.

Use layers of complicated transactions to distance the illegally gained money from its source.

You will also need to create an explanation, which will be believed as legal, for the source of the illegal funds.

Informal economy

Street traders, seasonal construction workers and temporary contractors constitute the World Bank's definition of the informal economy. These are the ten countries with the largest informal economy:

Country	Informal economy as a % of full economy
Georgia	67
Bolivia	67
Panama	64
Azerbaijan	61
Peru	60
Zimbabwe	59
Tanzania	58
Nigeria	58
Thailand	52
Ukraine	52

UK government salaries

For those whose rank is higher than MP the standard MP's salary is included in the wages figure given below.

Prime Minister	£189,994
Speaker	£138,724
Cabinet Minister	£138,724
Government Chief Whip	£138,724
Leader of the Opposition	£132,317
Minister of State	£101,713
Government Whip	£87,493
MP	£61,820

Equilibrium price in the prostitution sector

A 2002 paper in the *Journal of Political Economy* took an (academic) look at the sex market. It found that marital status, price, and male income determine the aggregate demand for commercial sex as:

$$D(y, p^*, p, n) = nd(y, p) + (N - n)^- d(y, p, p^*)$$

Where:
n = aggregate supply of commercial sex
$d(y, p)$ = demand of unmarried men
N = size of female population
$^- d(y, p, p^*)$ = demand of married men

Facts?

'I'd rather be vaguely right than precisely wrong.'
John Maynard Keynes

Advice for smugglers

Have you ever wondered which currency offers the greatest value when its highest denomination notes fill a briefcase?

Country	Currency	Value in briefcase US$m
Latvia	lat	13.80
Switzerland	franc	12.06
European Union	euro	9.70
Oman	rial	1.59
Azerbaijan	manat	1.51
Cayman Islands	dollar	1.47
Cuba	convertible peso	1.32
USA	dollar	1.23
Canada	dollar	1.20
Australia	dollar	1.18

Wife selling

Three men and three women went to the Bell Inn, Edgbaston Street, Birmingham in August 1733, and made the following entry in the Toll Book which is kept there:

"Samuel WHITEHOUSE, of the parish of Willenhall, in the County of Stafford, sold his wife, Mary WHITEHOUSE, in open market, to Thomas GRIFFITHS, of Birmingham. Value, one guinea. To take her with all her faults. (Signed) Samuel WHITEHOUSE / Mary WHITEHOUSE. Voucher: T. BUCKLEY."

Declining wealth of distinguished doctors

The *British Medical Journal* conducted research into the relative wealth in society of distinguished doctors, and found it to have declined over time.

In the period 1830-1879 the mean wealth of distinguished doctors at death, relative to average earnings of 2002, was £8 million, while in the period 1980-2001 their mean wealth was £597,000.

Adam Smith may well have been alarmed by this, as he wrote: *'We trust our health to the physician... Such confidence could not safely be reposed in people of a very mean or low condition. Their reward must be such... as may give them that rank in the society which so important a trust requires.'*

What does it cost - agriculture?

Milk, per litre	25p
Prime UK farmland, per acre	£8,000
Freshly calved heifer cow	£1,500
Rhode Island Red hen	£18
Rhode Island Red cockerel	£10
British Saddleback pedigree boar	£140
Three Wiltshire Horn Sheep, one ram, two ewes	£220
New Holland 1540 combine harvester	£3,500

Things money can't buy

'Money is not required to buy one necessity of the soul.'
Henry David Thoreau

Ten rules for trading

In *The Harriman Book Of Investing Rules* the futures trader, Neil Weintraub, lists his ten trading rules:

1 You will run out of money before financial gurus run out of trading ideas.

2 Never trust an economic boom fueled by consumer debt.

3 Trading without an exit strategy leads to disasters.

4 Never deal with a broker that won't give selling ideas.

5 "Money honeys" (female TV business news presenters) are pleasing to the eye but not your portfolio.

6 You can't eat a computer - have some "basic" stocks in your portfolio.

7 Day trading is like grabbing coins in front of a steam roller. You'll be flattened.

8 Know the difference between investing, trading and speculating.

9 You do not have to be in the market all the time.

10 By the time you hear news, the market has reacted and digested it many times over.

Trades on the NYSE

Number of shares traded (million)	Year when this first occured
1	1886
5	1928
10	1929
50	1978
100	1982
500	1987
1,000	1997
2,000	2001
3,000	2005
4,000	2007
5,000	2007

Poor in the USA

US states with the largest proportion of people in poverty.

State	Population below the poverty line (%)
Mississippi	22
Louisiana	19
New Mexico	19
Arkansas	18
West Virginia	18
Kentucky	17
Texas	17
Alabama	17
South Carolina	16
Oklahoma	15

The value of income reinvestment

The 2007 Barclays Equity Gilt Study showed the importance of income reinvestment (either in the form of dividends on shares or coupons on government bonds). The table below shows the nominal value in 2007 of £100 invested in 1899 in equities and bonds.

	Income not reinvested	Income reinvested
Equities	£13,311	£1,561,732
Gilts	£45	£20,132

NHS

The National Health Service in the UK is the third largest employer in the world. If it were a country it would be the 33rd largest economy in the world.

*

Hospitals are able to reclaim the cost of treating patients from the person who caused the injuries. In 2004-05 £117 million was recovered with this procedure.

*

Around £600 million a year is wasted by patients who fail to turn up for their appointments.

*

Each day there are around 40,000 meals wasted in the NHS, at a cost of £36 million a year.

*

The NHS spends around £40 million a year on paying for, or temporarily replacing, suspended staff.

*

The 82 highest paid staff in the NHS earn an average of £182,000. The starting salary for a nurse is £22,000.

**

600 acres of farmland

The table below shows the annual produce of 600 acres of land on a Welsh farm for three periods of three years. Though values rose from the first period to the second, as would be expected, they fell again in the third period. The farmer felt the cause was competition from Irish farmers.

Period	1787-90	1810-3	1830-3
110 acres Of Wheat	£637	£1,224	£561
70 acres Of Barley	£409	£693	£441
10 acres Of Oats		[consumed]	
12 acres Of Potatoes	£180	£240	£105
100 Fat sheep sold	£409	£270	£210
250 Sheep/lambs shorn	£47	£94	£94
2 Head of fat cattle each	£135	£300	£200
6 Cows	£112	£192	£128
100 Ewes, milked	£40	£70	£50
4 Horses sold	£44	£100	£60
30 Pigs sold	£52	£105	£52
30 Tons of Hay	£60	£120	£82
Total Produce	£1,852	£3,408	£1,984
Total Expenses	£792	£1,635	£1,231

A frank assessment

'Money never made a man happy yet, nor will it. The more a man has, the more he wants. Instead of filling a vacuum, it makes one.'
Benjamin Franklin

Losses of rogue traders

Trader	Company	Market	Year	Losses US$bn
Jerome Kerviel	Société Générale	Index futures	2008	7.1
Brian Hunter	Amaranth Advisors	Gas futures	2006	6.5
John Meriwether	Long Term Capital Management	Derivatives	1998	4.6
Yasuo Hamanaka	Sumitomo Coporation	Copper futures	1996	2.6
Robert Citron	Orange County	Interest Rate Derivatives	1994	1.7
Wolfgang Flottl and Helmut Elsner	BWAG	Forex	2000	1.9
Heinz Schimmelbusch	Metallgesellschaft	Oil futures	1993	1.4
Nick Leeson	Barings Bank	Nikkei futures	1995	1.3
Toshihide Iguchi	Daiwa Bank	Bonds	1995	1.1
Friedhelm Bruers	WestLB	Shares	2007	0.8

Richest people in Britain

With their wealth measured as a percentage of Net National Income, and then converted into the equivalent value today of this percentage, these are the ten richest people in British history:

Name	Wealth
Alan Rufus	£81bn
William of Warenne	£74bn
The Earl of Arundel and Warenne	£59bn
Robert of Mortain	£59bn
The Earl of Arundel and Surrey	£56bn
Odo of Bayeux	£56bn
John of Gaunt	£56bn
Henry of Grossmont	£43bn
Edward, The Black Prince	£35bn
The Earl of Warwick	£34bn

How the richest got their money

A breakdown showing through which sectors the 250 richest people in British history obtained their wealth.

Source of wealth	Number
Land/property	122
Merchant	53
Industry/textiles/coal/steel/transport	27
Finance/goldsmiths/speculation	26
Church/politics/judiciary/military	16
Brewing/food/retail	6

Mutilated banknotes

On submitting a damaged Bank of England banknote for
reimbursement it is worth bearing in mind that there are
criteria to be met before a cheque for the value of the
note is sent. The following will be assessed:

The size of the fragments.
*

More than half of the note should be present.
*

The presence or absence of some of the main features on
the note such as the serial number, the Chief Cashier's
signature and the promissory clause.
*

The declared cause of the damage.
**

One-armed economist

*'I want a one-armed economist so that the guy could never
make a statement and then say "on the other hand..." '*
Harry S. Truman

World's largest banknote

In 1998 the government of the Philippines issued the
100,000 Piso note which measured 356mm by 216mm
and became the world's largest banknote. It was released
to commemorate the centennial of independence from
Spanish colonial rule.

The height of the note is a little larger than the height of
this book, while the width of the note is *three* times
larger than this book's width.

Notes printed in America

Of the banknotes printed in America each year, 95% are used to replace notes already in circulation or notes taken out of circulation because of wear-and-tear. During the 2007 financial year 45% of the notes printed were $1 bills.

Original constituents of the FT 30 industrial index, 1935

Associated Portland Cement	Hawker Siddeley
Austin Motor	Imperial Chemical Industries
Bass	Imperial Tobacco
Bolsover Colliery	International Tea Co Stores
Callenders Cables & Construction	London Brick
Coats (J & P)	Murex
Courtaulds	Patons & Baldwins
Distillers	Pinchin Johnson & Associates
Dorman Long	Rolls-Royce
Dunlop Rubber	Tate & Lyle
Electrical & Musical Industries	Turner & Newall
Fine Spinners and Doublers	United Steel
General Electric*	Vickers
Guest Keen & Nettlefolds*	Watney Combe & Reid
Harrods	Woolworth (FW)

* Still in the FT 30 Index today.

An undertaking of great advantage

In *Extraordinary Popular Delusions and the Madness of Crowds* Charles Mackay famously tells of a company set up at the time of the South Sea Bubble whose business activity was described as:

'For the carrying on an undertaking of great advantage; but nobody to know what it is.'

*

Other bubble companies set up at the same time and which were subsequently declared illegal included:

'For the transmutation of quicksilver into a maleable fine metal.'

*

'For importing beaver fur.'

*

'For employing poor artificers, and furnishing merchants and others with watches.'

*

'For bleaching coarse sugars, without the use of fire or loss of substance.'

*

'For trading in hair.'

*

'For building and rebuilding houses throughout all England.'

*

'For a wheel for perpetual motion.'

*

'For drying malt by hot air.'

*

'For importing walnut trees from Virginia.'

*

'For buying and fitting out ships to suppress pirates.'

**

Five notable corporate blunders

In late summer 2008, amid concerns that fuel prices in the UK were becoming too high for people to cope with, a senior executive at E.ON said that in the event of a cold winter the high prices would mean the company made more money.

*

Gerald Ratner landed his family's jewellery business with £500m losses when he said that the company were able to sell products at low prices because the goods were 'total crap'.

*

The Barclays chief executive caused doubt about one of the bank's lead products - the Barclaycard - when he said he would advise his children not to build up big debts on credit cards.

*

EMI - the music company - upset people in Finland when their chief executive reduced the number of artists on a record label in the country, stating that there were not many people in Finland who could sing.

*

The brand director of the Topman clothing stores may have offended potential customers when he defined the company's target market as 'hooligans or whatever'.

**

Credit card ownership

The number of credit cards issued in the UK is 67,750,000. Of these, 62% had an oustanding balance on them. Of all balances on the cards, 73% were subject to interest charges by the card issuer.

International bribe payers index

Transparency International compile an index of 30 countries whose companies tend to use bribery and undisclosed payments when doing business abroad. The 30 countries are selected based on their importance as exporters of goods. Scores are calculated by completing a survey of business executives within each country. They are asked to rate how prevalent bribes have been in their experience in dealing with companies from the 30 countries. With a high score being good, the top ten countries from the most recent rankings are:

Country	Average score
Switzerland	7.81
Sweden	7.62
Australia	7.59
Austria	7.50
Canada	7.46
UK	7.39
Germany	7.34
Netherlands	7.28
Belgium	7.22
USA	7.22

The lowest ranked country of the 30 is India, with a score of 4.62.

National economic freedom

The World Heritage Foundation index of economic freedom takes ten categories and rates countries out of 100 for their standards in each. The categories include freedoms of trade, business and investment, and a positive influence by government on business and the economy.

The scores of the ten categories are averaged to give an overall indicator. The top ten (2008):

Country	Score
Hong Kong	90.2
Singapore	87.4
Ireland	82.4
Australia	82.0
USA	80.6
New Zealand	80.3
Canada	80.2
Chile	79.8
Switzerland	79.7
UK	79.5

Chip and PIN

The chip and PIN system was introduced to credit and debit cards to combat increasing fraud.

In the UK more than 97% of cards issued by banks now have a chip and PIN system.

This has made it possible for 185 transactions using the system to take place every second in the UK.

UK stock indices

FT Ordinary Share Index (FT 30)

The original industrial and retail index. Having only 30 companies it became unrepresentative of the market.

FTSE 100

The index of the top 100 capitalised stocks on the LSE. It represents 80% of the total market, by capitalisation.

FTSE 250

Like the FTSE 100, but it consists of the next 250 capitalised stocks, after those first 100.

FTSE 350

A combined index of the FTSE 100 and FTSE 250.

FTSE Small Cap

The FTSE SmallCap consists of the UK companies within the FTSE All-Share which are not large enough to be constituents of the FTSE 350.

FTSE All-Share

The FTSE All-Share aims to represent 98% of the full capital value of listed stocks. It includes FTSE 100, FTSE 250 and FTSE SmallCap stocks.

FTSE Fledgling

Those companies which do not meet the criteria for the FTSE Small Cap.

FTSE TMT

Companies in the technology, media and telecommunications sectors.

Public sector wealth

The TaxPayers' Alliance publish an annual list of salaries of public sector officials. The following is from their 2007 report.

Adam Crozier - of the Royal Mail - was the only person working in the public sector who earned more than £1 million. 66 people earned more than £250,000.

*

The 300 workers on the rich list had a pay increase of 13% from 2006 to 2007. This is considerably larger than the increase of 4% for the whole UK.

*

3% of the rich list are involved directly with the 2012 Olympic Games.

*

Gordon Brown is the 143rd highest paid person in the public sector.

**

Top ten highest salaried public sector workers:

Name	Organisation	Salary
Adam Crozier	Royal Mail	£1,256,000
Ian Griffiths	Royal Mail	£970,000
John Armitt	Network Rail	£888,000
Iain Coucher	Network Rail	£809,000
Mark Thompson	BBC	£788,000
Mike Parker	BNFL	£762,615
John Tiner	Financial Services Authority	£652,577
David Higgins	Olympic Delivery Authority	£631,000
Andy Duncan	Channel 4	£622,000
Jack Lemley	Olympic Delivery Authority	£611,000

January effect

Historically, the first trading week of the calendar year is a strong one in the stock market.

Revolution is closer than you think

'The way to crush the bourgeoisie is to grind them between the millstones of taxation and inflation.'
Vladimir Ilyich Lenin

United States Secret Service

The US Congress first authorised the issue of paper money in 1861 to help finance the efforts of the Union in the Civil War. This paper currency took the form of non-interest paying Treasury Notes called Demand Notes.

With the proliferation of paper currency came counterfeiting, and by the end of the Civil War between one-third and one-half of paper money in circulation was counterfeit.

To curtail this widespread counterfeiting the US Secret Service was created in July 1865, three months after the Civil War ended.

FTSE 100 Index

On 3 January 1984 the FTSE 100 index began, with a base level of 1,000. The highest value reached to date is 6,950.6, on 30 December 1999.

Importance of money

'It's important to me that money not be important to me.'
Les Brown

Foreign exchange and gold reserves

Country	US$bn	US$ per capita
China	1,534	1,157
Japan	954	7,472
Russia	476	3,358
India	275	242
Taiwan	275	11,943
South Korea	262	5,437
Brazil	180	962
Singapore	163	35,523
Hong Kong	153	21,930
Germany	136	1,657

Paper currency

The first notes with monetary value in the UK were issued
by goldsmiths in the 16th century. People would leave
gold coins with a goldsmith to keep them safe and were
given a receipt for the amount. Gradually these receipts
were accepted as payment for goods and services as the
bearer of the note was guaranteed the stated sum of gold
when it was presented to the goldsmith.

Warren Buffett and Berkshire Hathaway

$10,000 invested with Buffett in 1956 would have been worth $200 million in 2005.

*

Berkshire Hathaway's share price has increased annually by 25% on average.

*

It is estimated Buffett has a net worth of over $60bn.

*

Berkshire Hathaway HQ employs around 12 people.

**

That's enough money for me

'I've got all the money I'll ever need if I die by four o'clock this afternoon.'
Henry Youngman

What does it cost - travel?

To fill a Boeing 747-400 with fuel	£90,500
London - New York, 1st class aeroplane ticket	£4,518, or £1.31 a mile
London - New York, economy aeroplane ticket	£581, or 17p a mile
London - Edinburgh train ticket	£100, or 25p a mile
Moscow - Vladivostok train ticket	£400, or 7p a mile
New York - Los Angeles train ticket	£154, or 5p a mile
New Delhi - Mumbai train ticket	£30, or 4p a mile
One night, Mandarin Hotel, Tokyo, Oriental Suite, one person	£1,513
One night, New Road Guest House, Bangkok, one bed in a ten bed mixed dormitory	£2.48

Monopoly

Some facts about the board game Monopoly:

Parker Brothers rejected the Monopoly game when it was first presented to them in 1933, citing 52 fundamental playing flaws.

*

In 1941 the British Secret Service had John Waddington Ltd create a special edition for World War II prisoners of war held by the Nazis. Hidden inside these games were objects useful for escaping such as maps, compasses and real money.

*

The total amount of money in the original Monopoly game was $15,140, this has increased to $20,580 in the new edition (Sep 2008).

*

The twelve playing pieces that have been used include: a wheelbarrow, a battleship, a sack of money, a horse and rider, a car, a train, a thimble, a cannon, an old style shoe, a Scottie dog, an iron, and a top hat.

*

In Cuba, the game had a strong following until Fidel Castro took power and ordered all known sets destroyed.

*

According to Jim Slater there is a strong case for owning the orange sites, as players land on them more often.

*

The character locked behind the bars is called Jake the Jailbird. Officer Edgar Mallory sent him to jail.

**

The weight of money

The weight and composition of each British coin
currently in circulation is:

Coin	Weight	Composition
One pence	3.56g	Copper-plated steel
Two pence	7.13g	Copper-plated steel
Five pence	3.25g	75% copper, 25% nickel
Ten pence	6.50g	75% copper, 25% nickel
Twenty pence	5.00g	84% copper, 16% nickel
Fifty pence	8.00g	75% copper, 25% nickel
One pound	9.50g	70% copper, 5.5% nickel, 24.5% zinc
Two pound	12.00g	Outer: 76% copper, 4% nickel, 20% zinc Inner: 75% copper, 25% nickel

If you had one of each coin in your pocket, you would
have a total of £3.88 weighing 54.94g.

Performance of the FTSE All-Share Index

Data starts	1693
Largest one year rise	136.3% (1975)
Largest one year fall	- 55.3% (1974)
Average annual change	2.6%
Number of times it has risen 3 years in a row	65
Number of times it has risen 7 years in a row	8
Most consecutive rising years	13 (1977-89)
Number of times it has fallen 3 years in a row	29
Number of times it has fallen 5 years in a row	3

On shrimps and copper

A regular 75cl bottle of wine weighs around 1.25kg; the table below gives the current value of an equivalent weight of various commodities:

Commodity	Value (£)
Gold	21,867
Platinum	21,188
Silver	379
Tin	16.23
Nickel	15.34
Shrimp, Mexico	9.02
Copper	6.19
Meat, sheep	3.86
Meat, beef	3.03
Coffee, Arabica	2.62
Tea, Colombo auctions	2.43
Rubber, Singapore	2.39
Cocoa	2.28
Aluminum	2.24
Lead	1.56
Meat, chicken	1.44
Cotton Memphis	1.40
Zinc	1.40
Bananas EU	0.94
Oranges	0.92
Steel wire rod	0.92
Woodpulp	0.71
Urea	0.62
Rice, Thailand, 25%	0.53
Soybeans	0.45
Wheat, Canada	0.32
Sugar, world	0.26
Maize	0.19
Barley	0.17
Sorghum	0.17
Coal, Australia	0.13

Pension pot

In 2008 a 65 year-old man would need a pension pot of £525,000 to buy an inflation-adjusted annuity that would pay an annual income the same as the average wage of £24,908.

The long-term

The 2007 Barclays Equity Gilt Study showed the result of investing £100 in 1899 in the following asset classes.

Class	Value in 2007	Value in 2007 (inflation adj.)
Equities	£1,561,732	£25,022
Gilts	£20,132	£323
Cash (T-bills)	£17,856	£286

Note: gross income received reinvested at the end of each year.

Everyone should have some silver

Silver would be the money of last resort if there should ever be a severe global economic collapse. In this instance paper assets would be worthless, and silver would be the primary method of paying for goods and services. Gold would be a way of storing wealth, but it would be too high-priced for day-to-day use.

A parting thought

'Lack of money is the root of all evil.'
George Bernard Shaw

References

References

Books

Beresford. Philip and Rubenstein, William D., *The Richest of the Rich* (Harriman House, 2007).

Bernstein, WIlliam, *The Four Pillars of Investing: Lessons for Building a Winning Portfolio* (McGraw-Hill Professional, 2002).

Dickens, Charles, *David Copperfield* (Penguin Classics, 1994).

Eckett, Stephen, *The UK Stock Market Almanac 2005, 2006, 2007, 2008* (Harriman House).

Eckett, Stephen and Jenks, Philip, *The Harriman Book Of Investing Rules* (Harriman House, 2007).

Elliott, Matthew and Rotherham, Lee, *The Bumper Book of Government Waste 2008: Brown's Squandered Billions*, (Harriman House, 2008).

Friedman, Milton, *Capitalism and Freedom*.

Galbraith, John K., *The Great Crash, 1929* (Penguin Books Ltd, 1988).

Galbraith, John K., *The Affluent Society* (Penguin Books Ltd, 1999).

Groves, Francis, *Corporate Actions - A Concise Guide* (Harriman House, 2008).

Inman, Nick, *Politipedia: A Compendium of Useful and Curious Facts About British Politics* (Harriman House, 2007).

Keynes, John Maynard, *The General Theory of Employment, Interest and Money* (Palgrave MacMillan, 2007).

Lambert, Clive, *Candlestick Charts: An introduction to using candlestick charts* (Harriman House, 2008).

Leach, Robert, *The Investor's Guide To Understanding Accounts* (Harriman House, 2004).

Mackay, Charles, *Extraordinary Popular Delusions and the Madness of Crowds* (Harriman House, 2003).

Marx, Karl, *Das Kapital*.

Napier, Russell, *Anatomy of the Bear: Lessons from Wall Street's four great bottoms* (Harriman House, 2007).

Schabacker, Richard, *Technical Analysis and Stock Market Profits* (Harriman House, 2005).

Schroeder, Alice, *The Snowball: Warren Buffett and the Business of Life* (Bloomsbury Publishing, 2008).

Smith, Adam, *The Wealth of Nations* (Harriman House, 2007).

Twain, Mark, *Pudd'nhead Wilson* (Bantam Classics, 1984).

Academic papers

Edlund, Lena and Korn, Evelyn, 'A Theory of Prostitution', *Journal of Political Economy* (110, 2002).

McManus, I. C., 'The wealth of distinguished doctors: retrospective survey', *British Medical Journal* (331, 2005).

Websites

www.absolutefact.com
www.apacs.org.uk
www.bankofengland.co.uk
www.bba.org.uk
www.bbc.co.uk
www.bea.gov
www.bep.treas.gov
campus.murraystate.edu/academic/faculty/larry.guin/FinancialHistory.htm
www.cia.gov/library/publications/the-world-factbook
www.corporateinformation.com
www.currencyconverter.co.uk
deutsche-boerse.com
www.didyouknow.cd
www.ebay.co.uk
www.ebay.com
www.ecb.int/bc/euro/html/index.en.html
www.economist.com
www.fatf-gafi.org
www.frbatlanta.org
www.frbsf.org
www.feasta.org
www.foreignpolicy.com
www.fun-with-words.com
www.ft.com
www.genuki.org.uk
www.geocities.com/RodeoDrive/7503
www.goldipedia.gold.org
gold.yabz.com
www.guardian.co.uk
www.heritage.org
www.ibiblio.org
www.infoplease.com
www.imf.org
www.janeausten.co.uk
jak.aventus.nu/22.php

www.lightreading.com
www.londonstockexchange.com
www.mdleasing.com
www.measuringworth.com
www.moneyfactory.gov
www.namedevelopment.com
www.nationmaster.com
www.newyorkfed.org
nobelprizes.com/nobel/economics
www.nyse.com
www.nytimes.com
www.parliament.uk
www.photius.com
www.royalmint.com
www.royalmint.gov.uk
www.silverinstitute.org
www.sitmo.com
www.statemaster.com
www.statistics.gov.uk
www.telegraph.co.uk
www.timesonline.co.uk
tomchao.com/trivia.html
www.tse.or.jp/english
usgovinfo.about.com
www.usmint.gov
www.worldwide-tax.com
www.wordspy.com
www.xe.com

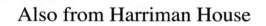
Also from Harriman House

The Origin of Financial Crises

Central banks, credit bubbles and the efficient market fallacy

by George Cooper

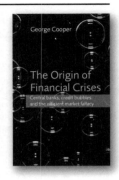

The Origin of Financial Crises provides a compelling analysis of the forces behind today's economic crisis. In a series of disarmingly simple arguments George Cooper challenges the core principles of today's economic orthodoxy, explaining why financial markets do not obey the efficient market principles, but are instead inherently unstable and habitually crisis prone.

ISBN: 9781905641857, Hardback, August 2008, RRP: £16.99

Never Mind Your Bonus

Here Is The City

by Vic Daniels

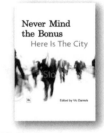

A compilation of the best, most amusing, entertaining or just plain eye-opening stories from the vaults of top financial website www.hereisthecity.com.

ISBN: 9781905641871, Paperback, November 2008, £14.99

Anatomy of the Bear

Lessons from Wall Street's four great bottoms

by Russell Napier

Looking at the four occasions when US equities were particularly cheap - 1921, 1932, 1949 and 1982 - Russell Napier sets out to answer these questions by analysing every article in the *Wall Street Journal* from either side of the market bottom.

ISBN: 9781905641574, Hardback, August 2007, £24.99

Extraordinary Popular Delusions and the Madness of Crowds

by Charles Mackay

Extraordinary Popular Delusions and the Madness of Crowds is often cited as the best book ever written about market psychology. This edition includes Charles Mackay's account of John Law's Mississipi Scheme, the South Sea Bubble, and Tulipomania.

ISBN: 9781897597323, Hardback, September 2003, £11.00

Dunces with Wolves

The third volume of the Bernard Jones Investing Diaries
by Nick Louth

When it comes to money, Bernard Jones is a bit of a dunce. The retired civil servant and amateur investor discovers that when share prices start plunging his wealth falls even faster. Bernard is the champion of all those who have lost out in the markets, and he is a refreshing anti-hero for our age of over-achievement.

ISBN: 9781906659011, Paperback, November 2008, £12.99

Corporate Actions - A Concise Guide

An introduction to securities events

By Francis Groves

Corporate actions have been sidelined for too long and deserve to be treated with more respect. Indeed no type of investment security can be fully understood without knowledge of its corporate actions. In this guide Francis Groves redresses the balance and gives Corporate Actions the attention they warrant.

ISBN: 9781905641673, Hardback, September 2008, £35.00

500 of the Most Witty, Acerbic and Erudite Things Ever Said About Money

Edited by Philip Jenks

A collection of the most memorable quotes on money, wealth and business success.

ISBN: 9781897597972, Paperback, April 2006, £4.99

Logic Problems for Money Minds

Revised edition

The conundrums, problems and riddles in this book have been collected by the editors over many years. The tests are designed to be fun and instructive - you will learn a lot about logical reasoning and you will have an arsenal of tricks to inflict on friends and colleagues.

ISBN: 9781897597965, Paperback, April 2006, £4.99

Politipedia

A Compendium of Useful and Curious Facts about British Politics

by Nick Inman

The ultimate quirky reference work for voters, students and those in the Westminster village. The book aims to capture the entertaining essence of politics without taking up too much of the reader's valuable time.

ISBN: 9781905641338, Hardback, August 2007, £9.99

Harriman's Financial Dictionary

Over 2,600 essential financial terms

by Simon Briscoe & Jane Fuller

A comprehensive dictionary focusing on financial and investment terminology and an essential reference work for anyone working in the City or related industries.

ISBN: 9781897597743, Hardback, August 2007, £16.99

The Midas Touch

The strategies that have made Warren Buffett the world's most successful investor.

by John Train

John Train introduces the remarkable story of Warren Buffett in this classic text. First published in 1987, *The Midas Touch* was one of the first books to recognise Warren Buffett's spectacular record.

ISBN: 9781897597293, Hardback, July 2003, £14.00

Shares Made Simple

A beginner's guide to the stock market

by Rodney Hobson

Shares Made Simple, written by highly respected financial journalist Rodney Hobson, tears away the mystique and jargon that surrounds the stock market. It takes you step by step through the most basic concepts of stock market investing.

ISBN: 9781905641451, Paperback, November 2007, £12.99

Harriman House

Harriman House is the UK's leading independent publisher of books about finance, business, investing and trading. The books listed here are just a small selection of our range of publications. They can be bought through all of the major high street and online book stores or direct from **www.harriman-house.com** or by phone on: +44 (0)1730 233870.

Corporate sales

We regularly work with corporate clients to offer bulk sale discounts on our titles or bespoke versions of our publications. We can provide branding or full customisation and can also offer individual fulfilment of products if required. As well as traditional printed books we also offer e-books, online education material and video content. Please call our special sales team to find out more: +44 (0)1730 269809.

Catalogue

If you would like a copy of our catalogue containing details of all our books, please call us on the same number, email us on enquiries@harriman-house.com, or write to Harriman House, 3A Penns Road, Petersfield, GU32 2EW.

Global Investor Bookshop

Harriman's sister company, Global-Investor, runs the well-known online bookshop of the same name:

www.global-investor.com/bookshop

The Gi Bookshop stocks more than 100,000 titles from all of the key UK and international publishers. We enjoy a reputation for keen prices, friendly service and quick delivery, and have many thousands of individual and corporate customers worldwide. Next time you are thinking of buying a finance book, please visit our site or phone our customer services team on +44 (0)1730 233870. We'd like to welcome you as a regular customer.